PRAIRIE takes us on a grand tour of the many faces and places that make up the Canadian Prairies. The dishes within these pages draw inspiration from the beauty of the changing seasons as well as the many different ingredients and cultures that make this region such a culinary hotspot.

From a comforting Cowboy Country Beef Roast with Smoked Garlic Gravy in the depths of winter to a fresh Saskatchewan Succotash Salad at the height of summer, Dan Clapson and Twyla Campbell have ensured there's a recipe for every time of year. *Prairie* also highlights the unique ingredients available in the region, with standouts like Sea Buckthorn and Thyme Posset, Haskap Flapper Pie Cups, and Hemp and Saskatoon Berry Granola Bars. Not only have they filled this book with produce-forward dishes, Dan and Twyla also share a mix of modern and traditional Prairie favourites—from Mrs. P's Perogies to Beet Mezzalune to Stir-Fried Tomato and Egg. Many of these recipes have been contributed by the talented purveyors and chefs in Alberta, Saskatchewan, and Manitoba, including Winnipeg's Adam Donnelly, Saskatoon's Jenni Lessard and Christie Peters, as well as Carmen Cheng and Garrett Martin of Calgary, to name only a few.

No matter the season, the Prairies are all about preserving every ounce of food, so of course there are also tons of helpful tips and tricks on reducing food waste. There's even a Staples chapter that will help you stock your pantry to keep you cooking Prairie-style all year long. Both a love letter to Canada's grandest provinces and an indispensable collection of over 100 recipes, *Prairie* is as inviting and bountiful as the region it celebrates and will appeal to anyone who has a connection to the Prairies and all their diversity.

PRAIRIE

PRAIRIE

SEASONAL, FARM-FRESH
RECIPES CELEBRATING
THE CANADIAN PRAIRIES

DAN CLAPSON AND **TWYLA CAMPBELL**

FOREWORD BY MAIRLYN SMITH

appetite
by RANDOM HOUSE

Appetite by Random House® and colophon are registered trademarks of Penguin Random House LLC.

Library and Archives Canada Cataloguing in Publication is available upon request.

ISBN: 9780525611929

eBook ISBN: 9780525611936

Cover and interior design: Andrew Roberts

Interior photography: Dong Kim

Interior photograph on page 2 by Ken Hughes

Interior photograph on page 72–73 from powerofforever/iStock/Getty Images

Printed in China

Published in Canada by Appetite by Random House®, a division of Penguin Random House Canada Limited.

www.penguinrandomhouse.ca

10   9   8   7   6   5   4   3   2   1

appetite
by RANDOM HOUSE

Penguin
Random House
Canada

To the women in my life who helped instill a love of cooking: My late mother Joan, grandmother Evelyn, and Deirdre.

I may not have appreciated it at the time . . . or realized it, but I sure do now.

This book is for you.

—Dan

To everyone with their hands in the dirt, I am grateful for your efforts. We couldn't eat without you.

—Twyla

CONTENTS

WINTER

FOREWORD

LASTING FRIENDSHIPS CAN HAPPEN ANYTIME and anywhere . . . you just have to keep your eyes open.

I first met Dan Clapson at a conference for food bloggers in 2013. Nervous about going alone, I nearly backed out at the last minute, but my husband convinced me to go. The conference went beyond my expectations. I met many wonderful Canadian food writers that weekend, but the highlight was meeting Dan. What stood out at that first meeting was Dan's sense of humour, his genuine kindness, and his unwavering passion for food.

A testament to friendships and their often-chance beginnings, Twyla and Dan's friendship began on a shuttle bus during a wine tour in the Okanagan, where they bonded over an Amanda Marshall song. They clicked that day and have continued to click. The two share a love for all things food, of course, but that love is rooted in their beloved Prairies.

Championing the endless bounty of locally grown foods that celebrate the unique terroir of Alberta, Saskatchewan, and Manitoba, Dan created the Prairie Grid Dinner Series, a travelling pop-up eating extravaganza serving local seasonal foods prepared by Canadian chefs. Twyla also joined the cause and became the series writer-in-residence for its inaugural voyage in 2017.

Choosing the foods that a region grows is an identifier. I'm a West Coaster, raised on salmon and raspberries. Living in Ontario introduced me to wild blueberries. Dan and Twyla have introduced me to bison, Saskatoon berries, sea buckthorn berries, and unique items like the roasted lentil and chickpea snacks from the Three Farmers in Saskatchewan. (As I'm the self-proclaimed "Queen of Fibre," they had me at "fabulous fibre-rich snacks"!)

Canadian cuisine is truly a melting pot of cultures. Sprinkle in our geographic diversity, season liberally with the wide array of ingredients we grow, and there's the possibility of a party happening on our plates every night of the week.

These two Saskatchewan-born food writers are on a mission to celebrate the Prairies. Let them take you on their food journey, which shines a light on one hidden culinary gem after another. I just know you'll be planning a road trip after you read this book.

Here's to local seasonal fare, my friends!

Peace, love, and fibre,

Mairlyn Smith, P.H.Ec.
Award-winning author and food personality

INTRODUCTION

DAN AND I HAVE BEEN reporting on the Canadian culinary scene for longer than Twitter has been around, which is quite a while. At the point of this writing, he and I are also two of the few remaining professional food critics in Canada.

We eat at restaurants (a lot!) and get paid to talk about our experiences. Obviously, we love food. We love to eat it, talk about it, and cook it too. With the food media landscape ever evolving, there may not always be a place for us to do our food critic portion of our work, but we'll be damned if we ever stop celebrating all that the Prairie food scene has to offer. To truly fall in love with where you're from, we have found that travelling abroad certainly helps! Let us explain . . .

We're both Saskatchewan transplants living in Alberta who have travelled the world for work and pleasure, separately and together, and what it comes down to is this: food is the focal point of our travels, and no matter where we've gone, the food we experience afar always connects us to home, from exquisite Chianina beef in Florence to an array of cheeses made by the owners of Pizza 4P's in Ho Chi Minh City. Our forays, without fail, remind us of our diverse culinary scene across the Prairies.

Just as the best dishes abroad are made with local, seasonal ingredients, so too are the ones made back home In 2017, Dan launched the Prairie Grid Dinner Series out of a desire to help unify the Prairie food community and help shine a light on the three provinces (Alberta, Saskatchewan, and Manitoba) as a whole.

We both knew that there were innovative people working tirelessly in the major cities—smaller ones too, as well as towns across the provinces—but it was seldom that these people were ever given the opportunity to interact with each other, let alone cook together. Dan asked if I would come along for the wild ride that would be the inaugural Prairie Grid in 2017 with chefs Adam Donnelly, Lindsay Porter, Christie Peters, and Jamie Harling . . . and I said yes with no hesitation.

That series ran each subsequent year, shifting course through the pandemic, but staying true to the concept of taking seasonal ingredients, putting them in the hands of talented cooks and letting them feed people. Dan decided that the hashtag #proudtobe-prairie was fitting for that first travelling dinner series, and it carried on every year that followed. But it also became a regular tag that we include in many of our social media posts outside of the series. We use it because it's true.

We're proud too, of this book. Some of the recipes are from chefs involved in those Prairie Grid dinners, others are from chefs we've written about, and a few are from friends we've worked with in the food industry on other projects. Dan and I have included our own family recipes and many new ones, too, that help showcase Prairie-grown ingredients in a new light, but regardless of who wrote the recipe, each one is intended for the home cook.

You will notice that some spring recipes call for frozen, dried, or cellared ingredients like root vegetables and dried fruit. That's because the Prairie provinces have a shorter growing season than most of Canada, and despite the notion of spring being the season of birth and renewal, not much grows here until June–rhubarb and asparagus being the usual mid-May exceptions.

Our parents and grandparents were conscientious consumers, and these crab apples didn't fall far from those trees, so you'll see that we include some tips for decreasing food waste and include the use of uncommon parts of the animal, like tongue, flank, and neck, in some recipes. Things that often get thrown away, like stale bread and bones, still have value, and we address that too.

Speaking of value, pulses are not only a significant source of vitamins and minerals, but they also contain a good amount of fibre and protein, which means you don't have to eat a lot to feel full. They also cost pennies per pound, so if you're looking to cut your grocery bill and/or your meat consumption, look for our recipes that use dried beans, peas, and lentils.

We hope that using this cookbook will inspire you to embrace the seasons, from a food standpoint. We hope the content within will open conversations around the table about the importance of supporting local producers–the ranchers and beekeepers; the pulse producers and mustard growers; the crop, dairy, fruit, and vegetable farmers–and those committed to working with the fruits of their labour: the grain millers and distillers; the brewers, butchers, and bakers; and the artisan cheese and sausage makers.

We have good reason to be proud of being "Prairie"; there is much to be thankful for. Now, let's get cooking!

Twyla and Dan

SEASONAL EATING: WHY WE CARE

EATING BY WAY OF SEASONAL availability isn't difficult, but it does take planning and a shift in how you think about food.

The planning part is easy. The Prairies' growing season is shorter than other areas of Canada, which means we need to get a bit creative with ingredients in the colder months. Freezing or drying seasonal berries allows us to use them in desserts in the off seasons, as Dan does with frozen Saskatoons in his fall crème Anglaise recipe, and with dried Saskatoons in his spring panna cotta dish. Cellaring and preserving vegetables are important too. Parsnips and sunchokes provide delicious comfort in the cold months when pulled from the cellar and roasted. Zucchini relish that was made in the summer, or beet pickles made in the fall, are bright and zesty sides to a dish like our Rutabaga, Ham, and Potato Bake (page 159), a perfect dish for any holiday dinner.

Don't have a root cellar? No problem. Late-harvest produce is available year-round thanks to indoor farmers' markets, where the vendors have done all the hard work for you. All you have to do is buy their food. And thanks to advanced greenhouse operations, you can still get locally grown foods like tomatoes, cucumbers, peppers, herbs, and even strawberries in the dead of winter, which means full-flavoured, vibrant dishes are easy to create any time of year.

And this is where the shift in thinking comes in. Food grown close to home and harvested at the height of its season delivers the best flavour and highest nutritional content it will ever have. That's because it hasn't been sprayed with anything to help it ripen or survive a trek–sometimes upward of five thousand kilometres–to a grocery store near you. Eating food that has been grown by people in your community who have made it their mission in life to feed you keeps dollars and jobs in the community. Despite the romantic notion often attached to living on a farm (often by those who don't), there is little glory in drought and hail and sixteen-hour workdays. The least we can do is support them by buying what they grow. If you talk to one of these farmers about how their beef is raised or why their chicken eggs cost more than those from a store, you will walk away knowing that the product you just bought was grown with love, care, and respect for the land on which it grew.

You don't have to totally give up lemons or lobster, but making the choice to eat what's grown in season and in your area not only helps strengthen your community, it also decreases the carbon footprint of food production and transportation around the globe. So think seasonal, support local, get cooking, and eat well!

HOW TO USE THIS BOOK

WE'RE NOT FUSSY, SO WE'VE kept this pretty simple. When you work with quality ingredients, you often don't have to do too much to them to end up with something fantastic. And even though we have recipes here from some of the top Prairies chefs, the recipes they've chosen are suitable for people who have plenty of kitchen savvy as well as those just learning how to cook.

We want cooking to be a fun part of your life. When opportunity presents itself, let the kids help or invite friends to join in with the duties. Food tastes better when it's enjoyed with others.

We also encourage you to consider other uses for what some might view as scraps or discards. Those items, like stale bread or vegetable peelings, have value, and we go into more detail about this on page 10. If you involve your kids in the cooking process, asking them questions like "What do you think we could use these carrot peels for?" or "What could we make with this dry bread?" helps them to feel a part of the process and will hopefully ignite a lifelong curiosity about food.

We support local, small-scale producers whenever possible. A list of producers we've used for this book can be found on page 276. Many of them have products that can be purchased online, so if you want something specific that we've used, please contact them.

To help with measurements and basic ingredients, and unless otherwise stated, keep this in mind:

- The butter we use is unsalted

- Flour is all-purpose

- Oil is canola

- Salt is kosher

- Eggs are large

We hope food will become a priority in your life, to be appreciated in all of its stages: the growing of it, the harvesting, the cooking, and the eating.

Take it easy, keep it simple, and take time to stop and smell the alfalfa.

WASTE NOT (FOOD OR MONEY)!

ASIDE FROM FOCUSING YOUR culinary energy and food consumption on using what's in season, there are other ways to be a conscientious consumer. The number one way is to avoid food waste, something that our parents and grandparents practised without even thinking, having had that ideology passed down from previous generations out of sheer necessity. When you don't have much, you can't afford to waste much.

Start by looking at food in two parts: what you can eat now, and what you can do with what remains—that means trim, peelings, and leftover parts that don't initially get eaten. For instance, what do you do with egg yolks when you've used the whites to make the Meringue Nests with Wild Blueberry Compote (page 246)? Use them to make custard (see page 55) or Hollandaise sauce. Egg yolks freeze remarkably well, as do cheese and cream, and speaking of cream, our recipe for ricotta is a good way to use up extra yogurt or cream that will soon expire. Making ricotta also gives you whey as a by-product, the necessary ingredient needed for our Braised Leeks in Whey (page 78) and our Leeks a' Whey au Gratin (page 82), which is similar to French onion soup and so perfect on a cold winter night.

Here are ten handy (and *easy*) tips to keep in mind if you're looking for ways to cut not only food waste but also food expenditures.

1. Got pickles in the fridge? Make the most of their brine by using it in virtually any savoury recipe that calls for vinegar or lemon juice. After all, the brine found in jars of (sour or sour-leaning) pickled vegetables is essentially flavour-infused vinegar. Hop on the pickle brine train with us and you'll never want to get off! Find us calling for the salty, flavourful liquid in recipes like Dill Pickle and Leek Soup (page 150).

2. Regrow the ends of vegetables like green onions, celery, carrots, and fennel by placing either the root ends or heads of the vegetables into a shallow bowl of water. After several days, you'll be impressed with the regrowth. They are the gifts that keep on giving and are great for garnishing dishes with fresh greens in the dead of winter.

3. Don't throw out Halloween pumpkins. Cook them and freeze the flesh to use in baked goods or soups. Simply quarter and seed the pumpkin, drizzle the flesh with oil, add some sea salt, and bake flesh side down on a baking sheet for 35 to 45 minutes at 350°F. And if you know of anyone who has livestock, they might take those pumpkins off your hands. Horses and pigs, especially, go wild for pumpkins.

4. Save the rendered fat from roasted meats or bacon and use it to fry or roast other foods. While you can store these fats in sealed containers on the counter or in a cupboard, it's best to keep them in the fridge. They'll last for up to a year and be less likely to go rancid if they're kept cool.

5. Don't throw out that bread! It can be made into stuffing, breadcrumbs for coating pork chops, or tasty soup dumplings like the ones in Butterball Soup on page 93.

6. Buy the whole bird and break it down. Save the bones and extra trimmed bits to make broth.

7. Freeze batches of seasonal fruit to use all year-round and turn them into easy-to-make syrups and compotes.

8. Make vinaigrettes and dressings from scratch (check out pages 267–269). Chances are you have all the ingredients already in your fridge or cupboard, and these dressings cost pennies per ounce, rather than dollars.

9. Eat more pulses! The recommended serving of cooked chickpeas is one cup (eight ounces), which works out to about $0.50 per serving based on a four-pound bag of dried chickpeas at $8.30 per bag. That one-cup serving contains roughly 14.5 grams of protein and 12.5 grams of fibre, so pulses (like chickpeas) are not only good for your wallet, they're good for your diet too. Check out our Hemp Hummus on page 141. The addition of hemp seed means you get the benefits of linoleic acid, which helps reduce cholesterol and blood pressure.

10. When it comes to fresh ingredients (we're talking about things you are unable to freeze and use later), only buy what you need. No further explanation needed.

SUMMER

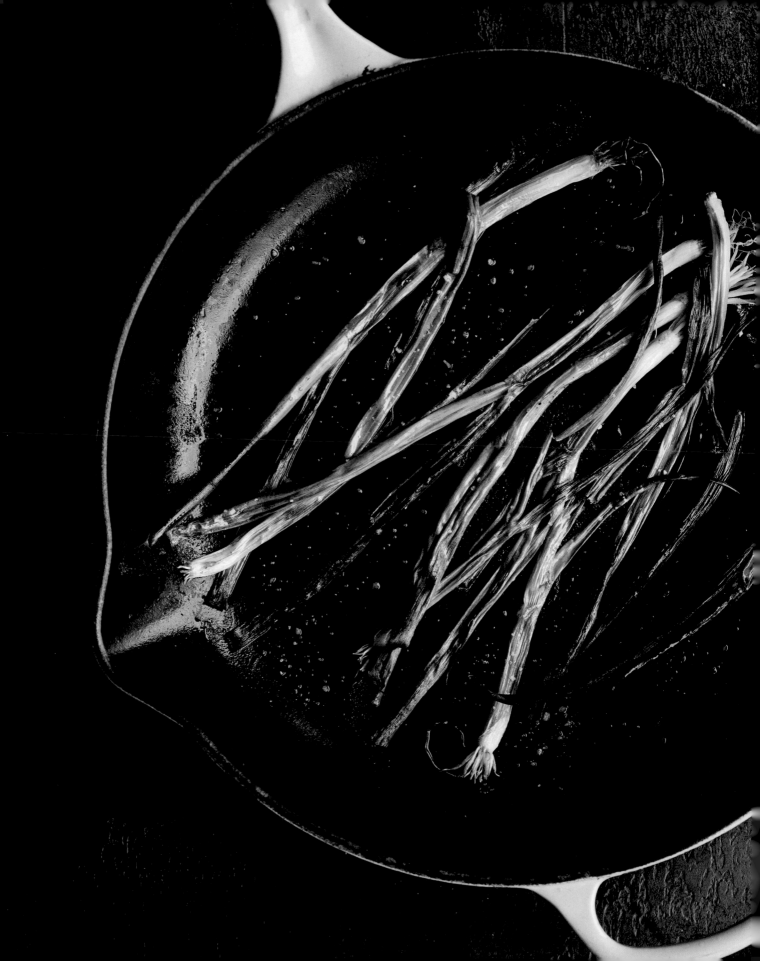

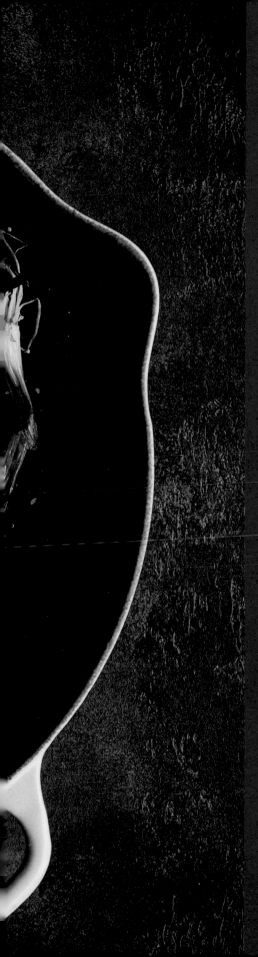

MAKE YOUR JOKES ABOUT FOLKS

in the Prairies nibbling away at cabbage all winter, but during the summer, just about every fruit and vegetable you can imagine is just a stone's throw away for us. By summer, gardens are really showing off their goods, and tables at farmers' markets are heavy with baskets of berries, including haskaps. These juicy purple berries are delicious on their own, but they also make spectacular jam and syrup.

And, tomatoes, glorious tomatoes, in colours that range from black cherry to neon orange. You can smell the sunshine in the vines that hold a half-dozen heavy red orbs. Those tomatoes will never taste better than now. Sweet corn, new potatoes, mountains of zucchini, and carrots so sweet and crisp you'll be snacking on them right out of the bag.

Get ready to grill those homemade burgers and raise a glass of mead (made with honey produced by more than 500,000 bee colonies in the Prairie provinces–about 80% of Canada's honey production). Our summer growing seasons may be short, but boy are they glorious!

COTTAGE CHEESE
GREEN GODDESS DIP

MAKES 2¼ CUPS

DC: Cottage cheese seems like the runt of the cheese family. Having a unique texture all its own, visually it isn't always for everyone. I've always had a soft spot for this cheese, and I am happy to enjoy it at its simplest: scooped into a bowl and topped with a generous amount of salt and cracked black pepper. In this spin on green goddess dressing, the cheese adds a beautiful creaminess and texture that you won't get with any other type of cheese. This dip is the perfect summer snack, so make sure to always have some chips or sliced veggies on hand for dunking.

2 baby cucumbers, coarsely chopped

¼ cup fresh chervil

¼ cup fresh flat-leaf parsley

¼ cup coarsely chopped fresh dill

¼ cup coarsely chopped fresh basil

½ tsp minced garlic

2 Tbsp pickle brine

¾ cup full-fat cottage cheese

¼ cup mayonnaise

3 Tbsp canola oil

Salt, to season

Sliced carrots, cucumber, fennel, and celery, for serving

Place the cucumbers, chervil, parsley, dill, basil, garlic, and pickle brine in a food processor or blender and purée until a relatively smooth green paste forms.

Add the cottage cheese and mayonnaise and purée again for 15–20 seconds, slowly adding the oil at the same time. Season to taste with salt, transfer to a bowl or sealable container, cover, and let the dip chill in the fridge until you're ready to serve. Best served same-day after chilling. Leftovers can be stored in a sealed container in the fridge for several days.

CRISPY CHICKPEAS

MAKES 2 CUPS

TC: Move over peanuts, popcorn, and potato chips, chickpeas are having their day! Many people are familiar with chickpeas being used in hummus, stews, or dishes like chana masala, or ground into flour for falafels, but the vast majority have yet to consider the chickpea as a snack—one that's filled with protein and fibre, and one that goes very well with a cold beer on a hot deck in summer. So, if you've got cans of chickpeas left over from the colder months—a.k.a. the soup and stew seasons—this recipe can help clear out the pantry. You might also be able to lighten up your spice collection, too, because almost anything goes when it comes to suitable flavourings for these chickpeas. Cinnamon, garlic powder, paprika, white pepper, and salt play well together. Add as much or as little of one or the other as you like. I use the sweet and savoury grilling rub from Watkins, but other pre-made rubs or spice mixes would work just as well.

1 can (28 oz) chickpeas, rinsed and drained

1 Tbsp canola oil

2 tsp seasoning (a packaged mix or equal quantities of garlic powder, mild paprika, onion powder, and white pepper works well)

½ tsp kosher salt

Preheat the oven to 400°F. Line a large baking sheet with parchment plus a double layer of paper towel.

Scatter the drained chickpeas over the paper towel and use more paper towel to pat the chickpeas dry. Pick up the corners of the paper towel and transfer the chickpeas to a bowl. Remove the paper towel from the baking sheet and scatter the chickpeas evenly back over the parchment paper.

Bake for 10 minutes to remove excess moisture. Drizzle the oil over the chickpeas, stir to coat, and return the pan to the oven.

Bake for 10 minutes. Stir and bake for another 10 minutes. Stir and bake for another 5 minutes, for a total baking time of 35 minutes. As soon as they come out of the oven, sprinkle with the seasoning and salt, and stir. Let the chickpeas cool on the pan and then transfer to a shallow bowl.

The chickpeas will keep in a closed container at room temperature for up to 4 days. They can be heated again in a 300°F oven for about 10 minutes if they need a fresh re-crisping.

SUMMER CUCUMBER KIMCHI

MAKES ABOUT 8 CUPS

DC: As Jinhee Lee is one of Calgary's most celebrated chefs, dining at her eatery is something I always look forward to. The JINBAR menu embraces seasonality with Prairie-grown ingredients while incorporating Korean flavours, making her approach to cooking a dynamic one. Here, she shares her recipe for summer kimchi. It's a perfect tangy complement to anything you might be tossing on the barbecue, from steak to tofu.

"Growing up, I would help my mother make kimchi with garden cucumbers on hot summer days. This was my first taste of fresh kimchi as a child, and I will never forget it. I love serving this with dishes as simple as steamed rice or noodles, but grilled meats too. Spicy, sweet, and savoury, to me this is the perfect summer side dish."
—Jinhee Lee, owner of Calgary's JINBAR

10 baby cucumbers, cut into 3-inch lengths and then quartered

1 yellow onion, julienned

1 carrot, peeled and julienned

¼ cup + 3 Tbsp granulated sugar, divided

1 Tbsp kosher salt

⅔ cup julienned daikon

⅔ cup julienned Asian pear

¼ cup water

½ cup fish sauce

½ cup gochugaru (Korean chili powder)

4 tsp minced garlic

Place the cucumbers, onion, carrot, ¼ cup of the sugar, and salt in a large mixing bowl and mix to combine. Let the mixture sit for 10–15 minutes, until the vegetables soften and release liquid. Discard the liquid.

Place the daikon, pear, water, and fish sauce in a blender and blend until puréed. Transfer the mixture to the mixing bowl of vegetables and add the gochugaru, the remaining 3 Tbsp sugar, and the garlic. Mix well and refrigerate until ready to serve.

You can eat this kimchi right away, but if you want to let the sour and umami flavours develop further, then let it sit for 1 day, covered, at room temperature, before serving. After 1 day, place in the fridge and eat within 4 days.

STOVETOP TOMATO CONFIT
MAKES ABOUT 3 CUPS

TC: The confit method, where a food is slowly cooked in oil over a low temperature, allows the fruit's sugars to come to the forefront and enhance those summer sunshine flavours even more. Small heirloom tomatoes will eventually split and break down in the pan, so they can be left whole. If you use larger tomatoes, it's best to scoop out the seeds and quarter them first. Confit tomatoes can be used as a quick sauce for pasta, added to soups or casseroles, or spread over cheese-topped crostini (see note).

1½ cups canola oil

1 Tbsp minced garlic

3 lb small heirloom tomatoes, left whole, or 3 lb Roma tomatoes, seeded and quartered

2 sprigs fresh rosemary

2 sprigs fresh oregano

Salt and pepper

Heat the oil over medium-low heat in a medium (5-quart) Dutch oven on the stovetop. Add the garlic and cook for 2–3 minutes, until tender. Add the tomatoes, rosemary, and oregano, turn the heat to low, and cook uncovered for 2 hours, stirring occasionally and mashing the tomatoes a bit when they get super soft. The end result should be a thick spread of silky cooked tomatoes.

Remove the herbs, season to taste with the salt and pepper, let cool, and store in an airtight container in the fridge for up to 1 month. There should be enough oil left to cover the tomatoes.

NOTES: *1. The thickened pulpy oil at the bottom of the jar is used to make the Roasted Tomato Vinaigrette (page 269).*
2. To use as a topping for crostini: Slice a baguette into ½-inch rounds, drizzle with olive oil, rub with raw garlic, and broil until golden brown. Flip and broil the other side. Remove and arrange the crostini on a plate with a small bowl of ricotta or crumbled goat cheese in the centre. Place 1 Tbsp of cheese on the crostini, top with 1 tsp of tomato confit, and finish with a pinch of Maldon sea salt.

GRILLED RADISHES WITH RHUBARB BUTTER SAUCE

SERVES 3–4

DC: Rhubarb never ceases to amaze me with its many uses and its ability to keep growing and growing . . . and growing. We can all agree that it is most frequently used in sweet applications like jams and pie filling, but do not underestimate the tart and tender vegetable's ability to lean savoury. The star of this recipe is the rhubarb butter sauce because of its beautiful brightness, but also its versatility. It can be used to complement an array of barbecued meats and vegetables in addition to things like summer squash or, my favourite underrated-when-grilled vegetable, the radish. It's so perfectly juicy and tender after being cooked that you'll wonder why you ever had radishes any other way.

Rhubarb Butter Sauce

1 Tbsp canola oil

2 cloves garlic, minced

2 cups thinly sliced rhubarb

⅔ cup dry cider (I use Uncommon Cider Co. Dry Craft Cider)

2 Tbsp local honey

½ cup melted butter

Grilled Radishes

12 radishes (tops trimmed, halved)

2 Tbsp canola oil

Salt, to season

Assembly

Crushed seed crackers or dry breadcrumbs, for garnish

Salt, to finish

Rhubarb Butter Sauce

Heat the oil in a medium pot over medium heat. Add the garlic and cook until fragrant, about 2 minutes.

Add the rhubarb, cider, and honey to the pot and cook, stirring occasionally, until the rhubarb has completely broken down, 10–12 minutes.

Remove from the heat. While whisking, slowly pour in the melted butter. The sauce can be served room temperature or chilled, but cover and keep in the fridge if made well ahead of time. It will keep in the fridge for up to 1 week.

Grilled Radishes

Place the radishes and oil in a large bowl and toss to coat. Season liberally with salt.

Preheat the barbecue to high (or 450°F if your barbecue has a more exact temperature control).

Cook the radishes directly on the grill for about 1 minute per side (see note). The radishes will fade in colour and turn some-what translucent in their interiors, with notable grill marks on the exterior.

Assembly

Spoon about ½ cup of the rhubarb butter sauce into the base of a serving bowl or plate and top with the grilled radishes. I like garnishing this dish with broken seed crackers or bread-crumbs–they add a great bit of crunch. Season lightly with salt and serve immediately.

NOTE: *If your barbecue's grill spacing is too wide for a radish, use a grilling pan or wrap the radishes in tinfoil.*

EASY CHEESY SQUASH BLOSSOMS

SERVES 4

TC: This is one of my favourite dishes and definitely not something I had growing up in Saskatchewan. The blossom was a part of the squash that people left to wither in the garden after the zucchini was snipped from its vine. It wasn't until I moved to Edmonton, a city with several Italian restaurants, that I first tasted *fiori di zucca fritti* (fried zucchini flowers) and fell in love with both the presentation of the dish and the flavour and texture combination of creamy cheese tucked inside lightly battered petals. Zucchini blossoms are available at farmers' markets through July and August, as well as at specialty grocery stores, depending on where you live. If you want to impress someone, learn to make this beautiful dish. The recipe is quite easy, and the end result will make you look super professional.

¾ cup all-purpose flour

1 cup sparkling water

½ tsp + ⅛ tsp salt, divided

1 egg

½ cup ricotta

½ cup grated mozzarella

1 Tbsp chopped fresh chives

1 Tbsp chopped fresh basil

⅛ tsp black pepper

8 squash blossoms

Vegetable or canola oil, for frying

Maldon sea salt, for finishing

Combine the flour, water, and ½ tsp of the salt in a large bowl and stir to mix until smooth. Set aside the batter.

To a medium bowl, add the egg, ricotta, mozzarella, chives, basil, the remaining ⅛ tsp salt, and the pepper and mix until fully combined.

Spoon 2 tablespoons of filling into each squash blossom and gently twist the top of the petals to close the blossom.

Pour enough oil to be 2 inches deep in a heavy-bottomed pan and heat over medium-high heat until the temperature reaches 350°F. If you don't have a thermometer, take a cube of bread and drop it in the oil. If the oil is hot enough, the bread will brown in about a minute.

Dip each blossom into the batter and then gently lay them one at a time in the oil, making sure they don't touch each other. You may only have room to do four at a time–if that's the case, fry these in batches. Fry for about 2 minutes, turning once, or until golden brown. Remove and drain on paper towel. Finish with Maldon sea salt.

TOMATO AND ROASTED GARLIC GAZPACHO

SERVES 4–5

DC: Warm summer nights were made for gazpacho. If you ask me, this is one of the best ways to use up the bounty of sun-kissed tomatoes you've got growing in the backyard. What helps this gazpacho stand out is a little roasted garlic, some hot sauce, and a superb black garlic vinegar from Alberta's Alchemist Vinegar. If you ever have the opportunity to pick up a bottle, I *strongly* suggest it! Add a splash of good-quality vodka to this recipe if you'd like to give the gazpacho a little extra zing.

1 bulb garlic

Canola oil, for drizzling

6 Roma tomatoes, coarsely chopped

½ English cucumber, peeled and coarsely chopped

1 Tbsp diced shallot

1 Tbsp Alchemist Vinegar Honey Blackened Garlic Vinegar (see note)

1 tsp local hot sauce of choice (I use Knockout Heat Co. Red Habanero Hot Sauce)

⅓ cup cold-pressed canola oil, plus more for garnish

Salt

Fresh garden herbs like parsley, dill, cilantro, or chives, for garnish

Preheat the oven to 350°F.

Carefully slice off the top of the garlic bulb so that all of the cloves are partially exposed. Drizzle lightly with canola oil, then wrap in tinfoil. Bake until golden and tender, 40–45 minutes. Let cool slightly before removing the roasted cloves from the peel. Discard the peel.

Place the tomatoes, cucumber, shallot, and roasted garlic in a blender and blend on high for 20–30 seconds, until the mixture resembles a smooth tomato sauce. Add the vinegar and hot sauce to the blender and then blend for 1 minute or so while slowly adding the cold-pressed canola oil. You will see the mixture increase in volume and lighten in colour. Once the mixture is fully emulsified, season to taste with salt.

Push the mixture through a fine-mesh sieve into a large bowl and discard the solids (see note).

Let the gazpacho chill in the fridge for at least 1 hour and don't remove until just before serving. You want this tasty, refreshing soup as cool as can be. When ready to serve, ladle into bowls, top with the fresh herbs, and drizzle with the oil to garnish.

NOTES: *1. Any type of vinegar can be swapped for the black garlic vinegar, but will have less depth. 2. If you do not have a fine-mesh sieve, you can skip that step and still end up with a delicious—though slightly less smooth—gazpacho.*

GOLDEN SUMMER MUSHROOM SOUP

SERVES 4

TC: Luckily, our farmers' markets and grocery stores usually carry a good selection of mushrooms all year round. The key ingredient in this recipe is the mild Hungarian paprika. It has a mild flavour compared to Spanish paprika, which is robust and smoky and can easily upset the balance of all other ingredients. Serve this with a leafy salad, a chunk of crusty bread, and an earthy pinot noir or tempranillo. A seat on the deck, string lights, one of the Eagles' greatest-hits albums on the stereo: all optional, but highly recommended accompaniments.

4 Tbsp butter

2 cups chopped yellow onion

1 lb wild mushrooms, sliced

½ cup dry white wine

2 Tbsp dry sherry or Marsala
    (Marsala has a deeper flavour)

2½ cups chicken or vegetable broth

2 tsp dried dill

2 tsp minced fresh thyme

2 tsp mild Hungarian paprika

2 Tbsp soy sauce

2 Tbsp all-purpose flour

1 cup whole milk

¼ cup sour cream

2 Tbsp apple cider vinegar

2 Tbsp chopped fresh flat-leaf
    parsley

To a large heavy pot or 9-quart Dutch oven set over medium heat, add the butter and melt it until it foams. Add the onions and mushrooms and sauté for 5 minutes, stirring occasionally with a wooden spoon. Turn the heat to medium-low, keep stirring, and sauté for another 10 minutes. Both the onions and the mushrooms should be a gorgeous golden colour.

Add the white wine and deglaze. Scrape up and mix in the browned bits from the bottom using a wooden spoon. When the wine has reduced by half, add the sherry and then follow with the broth, dill, thyme, paprika, and soy sauce. Give the soup a stir, bring to a simmer, and cook for about 10 minutes or until the liquid reduces by half.

Meanwhile, in a small bowl, whisk the flour into the milk until smooth, then add to the soup. Cook for about 3 more minutes or until the soup begins to thicken. Turn the heat down to low and slowly stir in the sour cream and vinegar.

To serve, ladle into bowls and top with the parsley. Any leftovers can be kept in a lidded container and refrigerated for up to 4 days, or frozen for up to 4 months.

GRILLED CARROTS WITH DILL PICKLE SAUCE GRIBICHE

SERVES 3–4

DC: As a kid, I remember adding hard-boiled eggs to empty pickle jars with lingering brine and waiting for several days with anticipation and impatience before being able to eat them. My "gribiche" uses some great Saskatchewan-made pickled eggs along with pickled carrots and green beans instead of gherkins and capers. Prairie-grown carrots are celebrated thanks to the juxtaposition of hot summer days and cool nights, which helps bolster their sweetness. The tangy condiment and the crisp, sweet carrots are a perfect match.

Dill Pickle Sauce Gribiche

2 pickled eggs, minced (I use Nanjo's Garlic Dill Pickled Eggs)

1 pickled carrot, minced (see note)

3 pickled green beans, minced (see note)

¼ cup cold-pressed canola oil

1 Tbsp yellow mustard

1 Tbsp apple cider vinegar

1 tsp honey

¼ cup finely chopped fresh dill

Grilled Carrots

12 garden carrots, greens trimmed but tops intact, halved

2 Tbsp canola oil

Salt, to season

Dill Pickle Sauce Gribiche

Place the eggs, carrot, beans, oil, mustard, vinegar, honey, and dill in a small bowl and stir to combine. Cover and chill in the fridge until ready to serve.

Grilled Carrots

Working in two batches, blanch the carrots in a large pot of boiling water for 1 minute and immediately cool in an ice bath or run under cold water. Pat dry.

Heat a barbecue to high (or 425°F if your barbecue has a more exact temperature control).

Place the carrots in a large mixing bowl, add the oil, and sprinkle with salt, then toss to evenly coat.

Cook on the grill for about 2 minutes per side, until the carrots have an al dente texture and a bit of char.

Transfer to a serving platter and top with a few liberal spoonfuls of sauce gribiche. Serve the carrots with the remaining sauce in a small bowl on the side.

NOTE: *You can find pickled carrots and green beans in Prairie-based grocers like Federated Co-op or Calgary Co-op. Any local farmers' market is sure to have them too.*

GRILLED GREEN ONION, GREEN BEAN, AND MOZZARELLA SALAD

SERVES 4–5

DC: It's pretty damn easy to whip up a salad in the height of summer. With amazing produce at your fingertips and plenty of sunshine, there's no reason not to take advantage of them. This recipe uses crisp green onions and crunchy green beans, and includes a great trick for marinating soft mozzarella cheese before assembling the salad. The marinated mozzarella really takes things to the next level taste-wise without requiring a ton of work, as does my subtly Prairie spin on a pistou, with all of its fresh herbs and sunflower seeds for added texture.

Sunflower Seed and Pickled Jalapeño Pistou

1½ cups unsalted roasted sunflower seeds

¼ cup pickled jalapeño slices

⅓ cup coarsely chopped fresh flat-leaf parsley

⅓ cup coarsely chopped fresh dill

⅓ cup coarsely chopped fresh basil

1 Tbsp pickled jalapeño pickling liquid

1 tsp honey

1 tsp apple cider vinegar

Salt and pepper

¼ cup canola oil

Marinated Mozzarella

2 cups 1-inch chunks of fior di latte mozzarella

3 Tbsp pickled jalapeño pickling liquid

3 Tbsp canola oil

1 clove garlic, smashed

1 handful fresh basil leaves

½ tsp chili flakes

Salad and Assembly

1 bunch green onions, grilled and coarsely chopped

1 lb green beans, cut into 1½-inch pieces, blanched and cooled

Salt and pepper

Sunflower Seed and Pickled Jalapeño Pistou

Place the sunflower seeds, jalapeños, parsley, dill, basil, pickling liquid, honey, vinegar, salt, and pepper in a food processor and pulse several times to combine. Continue to pulse and slowly pour the oil in until the mixture reaches the desired consistency–I like to do a fine chop on all ingredients and leave it all a bit more chunky for added texture, but blend as you like.

Season to taste with salt and pepper, then cover and place in the fridge until ready to use. This will last in the fridge for up to 7 days.

Marinated Mozzarella

Place the mozzarella, pickling liquid, oil, garlic, basil, and chili flakes in a small bowl and toss well to combine. Cover and place in the fridge to marinate for at least 30 minutes. Discard the garlic after marinating.

Salad and Assembly

Place the green onions and green beans in a large bowl along with $\frac{1}{2}$ cup of the sunflower seed pistou and the marinated cheese (including marinade). Toss well to combine, season with salt and pepper if desired, and serve.

GRILLED SWISS CHARD AND ZUCCHINI WITH RASPBERRY-MACERATED ONIONS

SERVES 4–5

DC: Raspberries have acquired a sentimental meaning to me, and I have raspberries tattooed on my shoulder as an ode to both my late mother and late grandmother. I also think of them every time I wind up with some in my kitchen. The dramatic red colour these raspberry-macerated onions yield is really something. Like, stop-you-dead-in-your-tracks something. Here, I use them with grilled zucchini and Swiss chard, but you can serve them with everything from grilled chicken to charcuterie.

Raspberry-Macerated Onions

1 cup fresh raspberries

1 yellow onion, halved and thinly sliced

1 clove garlic, smashed

1 Tbsp cold-pressed canola oil, plus more for plating

1 tsp honey

1 tsp salt

Grilled Swiss Chard and Zucchini

1 bunch Swiss chard, ends trimmed

1 medium zucchini, quartered and cut lengthwise into 1-inch-thick pieces

2 Tbsp canola oil

½ tsp salt

Raspberry-Macerated Onions

Place the raspberries, onion, garlic, oil, honey, and salt in a medium bowl and mix well with a spoon, mashing the raspberries as you go. Once the honey and salt have dissolved, cover and let sit for a minimum of 1 hour. (Leaving the mixture covered overnight at room temperature will result in more deeply coloured onions and a more intense flavour.) The onions will soften and take on the colour of the raspberries. They will keep in the fridge for up to 1 week.

Grilled Swiss Chard and Zucchini

Heat a barbecue to high (or to 425°F if your barbecue has a more exact temperature control).

Place the Swiss chard and zucchini pieces in a large bowl, drizzle with the oil, sprinkle with the salt, and then toss until evenly coated.

Place on the grill and cook for 3–4 minutes, turning at the halfway point. Watch the edges of the Swiss chard for over-charring—crispy leaf edges are okay, but the hearts of the chard pieces should still be tender. Coarsely chop the chard after grilling. Transfer to a platter and serve with the raspberry-macerated onions.

CUCUMBER AND FRESH HERB SALAD

SERVES 4

DC: Is there anything better than biting into a crisp, garden-grown vegetable in the height of summer? An ice-cold bevvy in the sunshine is right up there too, so multitasking and doing both will lead to near bliss. Since it's summer, it's likely pretty darn hot outside if you live in the Prairies. Therefore, this salad is best served as cold as possible. Maintain the crispness of the cucumbers by keeping them cool in the fridge and tossing in the dressing just before serving.

Cucumber and Pepperoncini Dressing

½ English cucumber, coarsely chopped

6 pepperoncini, tops and seeds removed

1 clove garlic

¼ cup coarsely chopped fresh mint

¼ cup coarsely chopped fresh basil

¼ cup coarsely chopped fresh flat-leaf parsley

1 Tbsp pickling liquid from pepperoncini

1 tsp apple cider vinegar

¼ cup canola oil

Salt

Cucumber Salad

1 long English cucumber, halved lengthwise and sliced into ¼-inch slices (see note)

4 baby cucumbers, cut as desired (see note)

½ cup coarsely chopped fresh mint

½ cup coarsely chopped fresh flat-leaf parsley

½ cup coarsely chopped fresh basil

½ tsp salt

Cucumber and Pepperoncini Dressing

Place the cucumber, pepperoncini, garlic, mint, basil, parsley, pickling liquid, and vinegar in a blender and blend until smooth. Continue to pulse the blender and slowly add the oil until the mixture emulsifies. Season to taste with salt and place in the fridge until you are ready to serve the salad. This dressing will keep in the fridge for several days, but will separate after approximately 12 hours (you can re-blend to combine again).

Cucumber Salad

Place the English cucumber, baby cucumber, mint, parsley, and basil in a large mixing bowl and season with the salt. Add about ½ cup of dressing and toss to combine. Add more dressing if desired.

NOTE: *In this particular salad recipe, I like to cut the cucumbers in a variety of ways. That way, even though your salad is one-ingredient-centric, it still can offer an array of textures. For example, use a vegetable peeler to create some long strips of cucumber in addition to chopping and slicing.*

ROASTED FETA AND VEGETABLE SALAD

SERVES 4–5

DC: Calling this a Greek salad would be blasphemy, I realize, so let's just say that this summer salad is an ode to the million Greek salads (both classic and non-classic) that I've eaten over the years. I've been making this salad for the past few summers and I love how the feta breaks down into a magical briny and creamy state after being roasted along with plenty of fresh vegetables. Roasting some vegetables and not others creates myriad textures with this dish too. If I ate this every day for the entire summer, I'd be a very happy camper.

Roasted Feta and Vegetables

2 Tbsp feta brine

3 Tbsp canola oil

1 Tbsp honey

1 tsp fresh oregano leaves

½ tsp salt

1 red bell pepper, seeded and chopped into 1-inch pieces

1 yellow bell pepper, seeded and chopped into 1-inch pieces

1 small red onion, coarsely chopped

1 cup ½-inch peeled and cubed kohlrabi

2 cloves garlic, thinly sliced

7 oz good-quality firm feta (I use Chaeban Firm Feta)

Salad Dressing

¼ cup feta brine

1 Tbsp apple cider vinegar

¼ cup cold-pressed canola oil

½ tsp finely chopped fresh oregano

Salt

Roasted Feta and Vegetables

Preheat the oven to 425°F. Line a baking sheet with parchment paper.

Place the feta brine, oil, honey, oregano, and salt in a large bowl and stir well to combine. Reserve a spoonful of this mixture for later, and then add the red and yellow bell peppers, onion, kohlrabi, and garlic to the bowl. Toss gently until evenly coated and transfer to the prepared baking sheet.

Clear a spot for the block of feta in the middle of the baking sheet, nestle it in, and bake for 20 minutes. Both the vegetables and feta should be tender and lightly browned. Set aside while preparing the remaining salad components.

Salad Dressing

Whisk together the brine, vinegar, oil, and oregano in a small bowl, and season to taste with salt.

Assembly

In a large bowl, combine the raw kohlrabi, cucumbers, and tomatoes with the roasted vegetables and feta, along with any residual pan juices, and toss gently. The feta should be soft enough to break down and coat the vegetables.

Assembly

1 cup peeled and thinly sliced
    kohlrabi

½ long English cucumber, sliced in
    half and cut into 1-inch slices

3 Roma tomatoes, halved and cut
    into 1-inch pieces

Transfer to a serving platter. Drizzle generously with the salad dressing and serve with the remaining salad dressing on the side.

STRAWBERRY, MINT, AND RADICCHIO SALAD WITH POPPY SEED DRESSING

SERVES 4

DC: A visually striking summer salad is an essential part of al fresco entertaining. Getting those "oohs" and "aahs" from friends when you set a dish down on the table doesn't need to be difficult—all you need are a few colourful (and in-season) ingredients, and a delicious salad dressing to make things pop.

"This salad dressing tastes like sunshine in a bowl! It is nicely balanced with the sweetness of the honey to tame the complex bitterness of the radicchio."
—Christie Peters, co-owner of Primal and Pop Wine Bar

Crab Apple Poppy Seed Dressing

½ cup honey

2 Tbsp Dijon mustard

2 Tbsp apple cider vinegar

4 crab apples, cored and peeled

½ tsp salt, plus more for seasoning

1 cup canola oil

½ cup poppy seeds

Zest of 1 lemon (optional)

Strawberry, Radicchio, and Mint Salad

2 medium heads radicchio, cut into bite-sized pieces, approximately 3 cups

1½ cups trimmed and quartered strawberries

⅔ cup coarsely chopped fresh mint

1 Tbsp picked fresh thyme leaves or fresh oregano leaves

½ cup coarsely chopped toasted hazelnuts

Crab Apple Poppy Seed Dressing

Place honey, mustard, vinegar, crab apples, and salt in a blender and purée until smooth. Continue to purée while slowly adding the oil to emulsify.

Transfer to a sealable container, and stir in the poppy seeds and lemon zest. Season to taste with salt and refrigerate until ready to serve. The dressing will keep in the fridge for up to 2 weeks.

Strawberry, Radicchio, and Mint Salad

Place radicchio, strawberries, herbs, and hazelnuts in a large bowl. Drizzle generously with the salad dressing (about ⅔ cup) and toss to coat. Serve immediately.

SASKATCHEWAN
SUCCOTASH SALAD

SERVES 4

TC: This is summer in a bucket—all the colours and flavours combined in one glorious salad that begs to be partnered with roasted, barbecued, or fried chicken. Saskatchewan grows a lot of great things (like me and Dan, for example), but they also grow an inordinate amount of pulses, too, including highly nutritious and extremely delicious black beans, which are a stellar addition to so many things, including this salad.

⅓ cup Herbed Buttermilk Dressing (page 267)

4 cobs corn

½ cup chopped red onion

1 cup canned black beans, rinsed

1 cup halved cherry tomatoes

½ cup cubed or crumbled feta

½ cup cubed cucumber

1 head bibb lettuce

¼ cup ribboned fresh basil

Make the buttermilk dressing first so the flavours have time to develop.

Bring a large pot of salted water to a boil and add the cobs of corn. Cook for 10 minutes, remove from the heat, and allow to cool.

Use a sharp knife to remove the kernels, collecting them in a large bowl. Add the onion, beans, tomatoes, feta, and cucumber. Add ¼ cup of the dressing and gently mix.

Arrange the salad over the leaves of lettuce and scatter with the basil.

LENTIL SALAD WITH ROASTED CARROTS AND CRISPY CHICKPEAS

SERVES 4

TC: There is a lot going on in this colourful, healthy salad that eats like a meal. Protein-packed lentils and a bucket of summer vegetables and herbs deliver bold, fresh flavours in every bite. The textures keep things interesting, too, with creamy bits of goat cheese nestled against crispy chickpeas. It's a salad, yes, but one that, say, a superhero might eat.

2 cups dried green lentils

3 rainbow carrots, peeled and sliced into ¾-inch-thick rounds

½ Tbsp canola oil

½ tsp salt

¼ tsp freshly ground black pepper

2 cups cherry or grape tomatoes

1 baby English cucumber, chopped

½ cup chopped red onion

½ cup chopped fresh mint

½ cup chopped fresh flat-leaf parsley

½ cup Apple Cider Vinaigrette (page 269)

½ cup crumbled goat cheese

½ cup Crispy Chickpeas (page 18)

Preheat the oven to 375°F and line a baking sheet with parchment paper.

Put the lentils in a medium saucepan and add enough water to cover by about 2½ inches. Bring to a boil, then reduce the heat, cover, and simmer for 40 minutes or until tender. When the lentils are done, strain using a colander. Let cool water run over the strained lentils for about a minute. Stir and set aside.

Place the carrots in a bowl and drizzle with the oil, then sprinkle with the salt and pepper. Stir to coat and arrange the carrots in a single layer on the baking sheet. Roast for 15 minutes, or just until tender. Let cool.

To a large bowl, add the cooled lentils, carrots, tomatoes, cucumber, onion, mint, and parsley, and dress with the vinaigrette. Portion out servings, and top with the goat cheese and chickpeas.

VIETNAMESE-STYLE BISON AND PORK PATTIES WITH VERMICELLI

SERVES 4

DC: My good friend Linh Phan runs a tour company in Saigon—aptly titled Hidden Saigon—and has helped me discover the dynamic food community within the vibrant Vietnamese metropolis. Preparations of bún chả can vary from grilled pieces of pork to seasoned and formed pork patties, but whatever way it is served, it always hits the spot. My recipe calls for ground bison and honey for the patties to give it a Prairie spin. It may surprise you to know that kohlrabi is everywhere in Vietnam and is found in many sauces that accompany noodle dishes like this one.

Dipping Sauce

2 Tbsp fish sauce

2 Tbsp rice vinegar

⅓ cup water

¼ cup granulated sugar

1 clove garlic, very thinly sliced

1 pinch chili flakes

½ cup very thinly sliced peeled kohlrabi

Marinade and Patties

1 tsp maple syrup

1 tsp canola oil

1 tsp fish sauce

½ tsp ground black pepper

1 shallot, minced

1 clove garlic, minced

¼ lb ground pork

¼ lb ground bison

Assembly

Lettuce leaves

Fresh herbs like mint, basil, and dill

1 package (14–16 oz) vermicelli noodles, cooked

Dipping Sauce

Combine the fish sauce, vinegar, water, and sugar in a small pot and bring to a boil. Remove from the heat, add the garlic, chili flakes, and kohlrabi, and let sit until ready to serve.

Marinade and Patties

Heat the maple syrup and oil in a small pan or pot on medium-high heat. Cook until the syrup darkens in colour, about 3 minutes. Once the syrup has caramelized, remove from the heat and add the fish sauce, black pepper, shallot, and garlic. Stir to combine and allow to cool.

Use your hands to mix the ground pork and bison and the marinade in a large bowl and let chill in the fridge for a minimum of 20 minutes. Once marinated, form the mixture into small patties, approximately 1 inch long and ½ inch wide.

Cook the patties on a well-oiled hot grill or in a hot pan until well browned on each side, about 1 minute per side.

Assembly

To serve, place the noodles, lettuce, and herbs on one side of the plate, with the patties on the other side. Portion the dipping sauce into four small bowls and serve on the side.

FARMSTEAD FLANK STEAK

SERVES 2

TC: Flank steak is an underrated and underappreciated cut of meat. We hope to change that. This long, lean cut comes from the abdominal wall of the animal, and if it is improperly prepared, you'll have a very poor flank experience. The key is to marinate the steak for 4–12 hours in a combination of fat, acid, salt, and sugar. Any seasonings you add (cumin, garlic, fennel, etc.) depend on your personal preference. The key to cooking a flank steak is to cook it hot and fast, or low and slow. The key to eating it is to cut it on the diagonal after it's cooked. That way, you make short work of the long muscle fibres.

The recipe below is basic; the meat I work with, on the other hand, is not. My source rarely varies from Lakeside Farmstead, north of Edmonton. While most of the Holstein cattle are used for the farm's dairy production, a good portion of the herd are raised for beef—some kept as purebred, others crossed with wagyu. Out of the thousands of pounds I've tasted over the years (not really joking), not one of them disappointed.

½ cup canola oil

¼ cup balsamic vinegar

1½ Tbsp Worcestershire sauce

2 Tbsp brown sugar

1 tsp onion powder

2 cloves garlic, crushed

1 tsp kosher salt

¼ tsp freshly ground black pepper

1 lb flank steak

Maldon sea salt, for finishing

Combine the oil, vinegar, Worcestershire sauce, brown sugar, onion powder, garlic, salt, and pepper in a bowl and whisk to incorporate. Put the steak in a large zip-lock bag and add the marinade. Seal, then turn the bag over a few times to make sure the meat gets well coated. Refrigerate for up to 12 hours.

Heat a barbecue to medium-high and cook the steak for 3 minutes per side, turning four times to get some crosshatch grill marks, for a total cooking time of up to 12 minutes for medium-rare. Use a meat thermometer for best results. A medium-rare steak should be taken off when the internal temperature is 135°F and rested for 5 minutes.

Place the meat on a cutting board, cut across the grain, and portion out onto two plates. Finish with Maldon sea salt. This is wonderful paired with the Grilled Green Onion, Green Bean, and Mozzarella Salad (page 34).

RYE WHISKY SOUFFLÉ PANCAKES

SERVES 4

DC: When Twyla and I were discussing what pancake recipe to add to our cookbook, we knew there was only one person to ask: Scott Redekopp. This 2018 Prairie Grid Dinner Series alumnus is also credited with popularizing soufflé pancakes in Calgary. The weekend brunch at Yellow Door Bistro, located inside Hotel Arts, rose to fame largely because of these fluffy, mile-high pancakes. The soufflé pancakes have seen many iterations over the years, but this recipe is a perfect ode to Alberta's most famous festival and its signature pancake breakfasts. It's also one of the chef's favourites.

"The Calgary Stampede is always a fun time of year and pancakes are a daily staple throughout. Soufflé pancakes were a signature dish of Yellow Door Bistro for many years and, surprisingly, they are easy enough to make at home if you're willing to commit a bit of time to the process." **—Scott Redekopp, executive sous chef at Hotel Arts**

Rye Whisky Caramel Sauce

1 cup heavy (35%) cream

¼ cup + 1 Tbsp good-quality Alberta rye whisky

3 Tbsp maple syrup

1 cup granulated sugar

½ cup packed brown sugar

1 Tbsp sea salt

¼ cup butter, cut into 4 equal cubes

2 strips cooked crispy bacon, finely chopped

Rye Whisky Caramel Sauce

In a large bowl, combine the heavy cream, whisky, and maple syrup.

In a heavy-bottomed large pot, combine the granulated sugar and brown sugar and place over medium-high heat, stirring occasionally to prevent burning. The sugars will start to melt and deepen in colour. Once the colour of the sugar is a dark amber, remove from the heat and add the cream mixture. The cream will make the sugar bubble hard. Just allow the bubbling to subside and then place the pot back on the heat. Stir the mixture until it has become smooth, and then add the salt and cubed butter. Keep stirring until the mixture is smooth.

Remove from the heat, stir in the chopped bacon, and cover to keep warm.

continued on next page

Rye Whisky Pancakes

1 cup half and half cream

3 Tbsp instant coffee granules

1 cup good-quality Alberta rye
    whisky, divided

4 eggs

¼ cup granulated sugar

¼ cup melted or brown butter

1 cup rye flour

1 cup all-purpose flour

1 Tbsp baking powder

Canola oil or melted butter, for
    cooking pancakes

Assembly

8 strips cooked crispy bacon

Rye Whisky Pancakes

In a small saucepan or pot over medium-high heat, combine the cream and instant coffee. Bring to a simmer and allow to simmer for 1 minute. Remove from the heat and refrigerate for 10 minutes to cool. When the mixture has cooled, add ½ cup of the whisky (and try not to drink the rest!).

Separate the egg whites and egg yolks cleanly into two separate large bowls. Whisk the egg whites until stiff peaks form—the whites should stand straight up on the whisk.

Whisk the egg yolks with the granulated sugar. While whisking, add the butter and the remaining ½ cup rye whisky. Gently whisk the rye flour, all-purpose flour, and baking powder into the egg yolk mixture until combined and stiff. Gently fold in the egg whites until well incorporated.

Heat a non-stick pan over medium heat and add some oil to grease the pan. Place ½ cup portions of the batter in the pan. Be sure to leave 2 inches or so of space between pancakes, otherwise you will end up making one large pancake. Once bubbles are visibly popping up in the centre of the batter, flip the pancake and continue to cook for another 3–4 minutes.

Assembly

Gently place 2 pieces of crispy bacon in between pancake stacks. Top generously with whisky caramel sauce and go to town!

HASKAP FLAPPER PIE CUPS

SERVES 4

TC: Flapper pie is a favourite Prairie dessert that features a graham cracker crumb base with a custard filling and meringue topping. At seven years old, I took over the flapper pie–making duty from Mom, but back then we used Bird's custard powder to make the pudding. I can only assume this quick mix was one of those time savers of the 1960s, marketed to women in an effort to ease their workload. A wee bit of nostalgia certainly kicks in whenever I see that bright red, blue, and yellow container on a store shelf, but for this recipe, I'm going with made-from-scratch custard.

This "deconstructed flapper pie" features a dollop of haskap compote as a bonus. Haskap berries are native to northern Japan and Russia, but they now grow across Canada, with a good concentration of them on the Prairies. The flavour of this elongated purple fruit is a combination of raspberry and blueberry with undertones of concord grape and black currant.

This recipe has all the good things: sweet fruit with a bit of tang, creamy custard, a buttery base with a hit of salt, and a light-as-a-feather crunchy topping courtesy of our Meringue Nests with Wild Blueberry Compote (page 246). Oh, and it looks good too.

Graham Cracker Base

20 graham crackers

⅓ cup melted salted butter

⅓ cup granulated sugar

Custard

2 egg yolks

2 cups whole milk

2 Tbsp cornstarch

⅓ cup granulated sugar

1 tsp pure vanilla extract

Graham Cracker Base

In a food processor, pulse the graham wafer crackers into fine crumbs. Transfer the crumbs to a medium bowl, add the melted butter and sugar, and mix with a spoon until combined. Portion out about ½ cup per serving into four dessert bowls and set aside until ready to use.

Custard

Lightly mix the egg yolks and set aside.

To a medium saucepan, add the milk and cornstarch and whisk until smooth. Add the sugar and vanilla, and stir to combine. Place the pan over medium heat, slowly add the yolks to the

continued on next page

Haskap Compote

1 cup haskap berries, fresh or frozen

2 Tbsp water

2 Tbsp granulated sugar

1 tsp fresh lemon juice

½ tsp vanilla

½ tsp cornstarch dissolved in ½ Tbsp of water

Assembly

1 cup crushed baked meringue (½ batch of meringue nest from Meringue Nests with Wild Blueberry Compote, page 246)

Fresh mint, for garnish (optional)

mixture, and whisk until thickened, about 2 minutes. Remove from the heat and let cool for 15 minutes, stirring every few minutes. Cover and refrigerate until needed.

Haskap Compote

Mix together the berries, water, sugar, lemon juice, vanilla, and cornstarch in a small saucepan and bring to a boil. Turn the heat down and simmer for 10 minutes or until thickened. The compote should be saucy but still have noticeable chunks of fruit. Can be used warm, room temperature, or cool for this recipe.

Assembly

Add one-quarter of the custard followed by one-quarter of the compote to the portioned-out bowls of graham cracker crumbs. Top with crushed meringue and garnish with mint.

NOTE: *If you need to make fresh meringues for this recipe, then plan ahead, because meringues need at least 3 hours in the oven. Also, the egg yolks that you (hopefully) froze after making those meringues can be called into service now to make the custard—you just need to take them out of the fridge beforehand and let them come to room temperature.*

SEA BUCKTHORN AND THYME POSSET

SERVES 6

DC: This little-known, age-old dessert has British roots and is an absolute breeze to make. The combination of hot cream, an acidic liquid, and a little sweetener is nothing short of magical. Posset is traditionally made with lemon, but here the juice of intensely tart sea buckthorn berries makes for a great—and *very* Prairie—substitution. Sea buckthorn berries can be found in the wild, of course, but because of their trees' sturdy root systems, they became a favourite of farmers to plant as shelter belts for crops. Last but not least, sea buckthorn adds a striking hue to the completed dessert.

¾ cup granulated sugar

1 cup Nvigorate Seabuckthorn Splash (or Sea Buckthorn Juice, page 260, see note)

1-inch piece ginger root, peeled

2 sprigs fresh thyme

2¼ cups heavy (35%) cream

1 pinch sea salt

Fresh sea buckthorn berries, for garnish

1 Tbsp fresh thyme leaves, for garnish

NOTE: *If using the Sea Buckthorn Juice on page 260 in this recipe, the posset will be noticeably tarter. You can add 1 Tbsp of granulated sugar to the juice to balance this out if desired, but regardless, the end result will still be a tasty one!*

To a large pan, add the granulated sugar, Seabuckthorn Splash, ginger, and thyme. Stir and bring to a simmer over medium-high heat. Once the sugar has dissolved, remove from the heat and let the mixture steep for 10 minutes to let the aromatics infuse. Strain the mixture through a fine-mesh sieve into a medium bowl and discard the ginger root and thyme sprigs.

Place the cream and salt in a medium pot over medium-high heat and heat until just about to simmer, 4–5 minutes. Reduce the heat to low and let the cream cook, stirring frequently to keep from scalding, for 5 minutes. Add the sea buckthorn mixture to the pot and stir. The contents of the pot will appear notably thickened. Continue to cook while stirring for about 1 minute.

Remove from the heat and divide the mixture between six ramekins or small heat-safe bowls. Let sit until back at room temperature and then place uncovered in the fridge to cool and set, approximately 4 hours.

When ready to serve, remove the posset from the fridge and top with a few sea buckthorn berries and thyme. The posset can be made up to 5 days in advance. If being made in advance, cover with plastic wrap until you're ready to garnish and serve.

SPICED STRAWBERRIES

MAKES 2 CUPS

TC: This quick strawberry sauce can be made with fresh summer berries, or with ones you have stashed in the freezer. Freezing berries picked at the height of their season is easy—just rinse them, scatter them on a baking sheet lined with parchment paper, pop the sheet in the freezer, and then transfer the berries to containers once they're frozen solid. Use this recipe to make a sauce that is wonderful over yogurt or ice cream. It also makes a great addition to the picnic basket, to pair with some brie cheese alongside a handful of plain crackers and a Canadian dry white wine.

The elixir that results after the stewed fruit is strained can be used to make Strawberry Vinaigrette (page 268).

1 lb strawberries, rinsed, hulled, and quartered

¾ cup unoaked white wine (pinot gris, sauvignon blanc, or dry riesling work well)

2 Tbsp creamed or liquid honey

1 tsp cinnamon

3 cloves

Place the strawberries, wine, honey, cinnamon, and cloves in a medium saucepan. Bring to a boil, turn to low, and simmer for 30 minutes, stirring occasionally.

Remove from the heat and discard the cloves. Pour the stewed fruit through a mesh sieve placed over a bowl and reserve the liquid. Save this elixir to use for salad dressings. The berries should have broken down into bite-sized pieces, but if large chunks remain, give them a few mashes with a potato masher to break them down some more.

Keep the stewed strawberries and the elixir in separate sealable jars in the fridge. Both can be frozen for up to 3 months, or kept in the fridge for up to 2 weeks.

RASPBERRY CLAFOUTIS

SERVES 6-8

TC: The late chef Gail Hall was one of Edmonton's most outspoken supporters of seasonal eating and small-scale producers. This clafoutis recipe was one of the first dishes she taught people to make at her loft cooking school in downtown Edmonton, located on the same street as the farmers' market. After picking up the fresh ingredients, Gail would take her students back to the loft to eat, cook, and laugh together for most of the day. Her clafoutis recipe was made with plums, but we're making this beautiful dessert with a different summer fruit, letting raspberries be the stars of the show. Gail would have been totally fine with that.

2½ cups fresh raspberries

5 Tbsp granulated sugar, divided

¾ cup whole milk

3 eggs

1 Tbsp amaretto liqueur

2 Tbsp melted butter

¾ cup all-purpose flour

½ tsp baking powder

¼ tsp salt

1 cup heavy (35%) cream

2 Tbsp icing sugar

½ tsp pure vanilla extract

½ tsp cinnamon

Preheat the oven to 375°F and butter a 10-inch pie plate.

Distribute the raspberries in the prepared pie plate and sprinkle with 2 Tbsp of the sugar.

In a small bowl, beat together the milk, eggs, amaretto, and butter. Add the flour, another 2 Tbsp of sugar, baking powder, and salt and beat to a smooth batter. Pour over the raspberries and bake until golden brown and set in the middle, about 30 minutes. The batter will puff slightly.

While the batter is baking, prepare the whipped cream. If using a stand mixer or hand mixer, pour the cream into a large bowl, add the icing sugar and vanilla, and whisk on medium-high speed for about 4 minutes, until medium firm peaks are formed. If using an immersion blender, pour the cream, sugar, and vanilla into a 4-cup jar and blend for the same time, until medium peaks are formed. Cover the container with plastic wrap and place in the fridge until ready to use.

When the clafoutis has finished baking, remove it from the oven and sprinkle it with the cinnamon and the remaining 1 Tbsp sugar. Let cool for 15 minutes before cutting into wedges. Serve with the whipped cream.

HASKAP SMASH

SERVES 1

TC: Sporting a glorious dark-purple hue, this cocktail tastes as good as it looks—sparkling, tangy, and refreshing all in one! Use a gin that has a citrus-forward flavour profile (as opposed to a vegetal or herbaceous profile) to complement the fruit in this recipe.

Juice of ½ lime

¼ cup fresh haskap berries

1 oz Haskap Simple Syrup
   (page 274)

2 oz gin

4–6 oz club soda

1 sprig mint

To a tall glass, add the lime juice and berries. Muddle gently with the back of a spoon. Add the simple syrup and stir. Fill the glass three-quarters of the way with ice, add the gin, top with club soda, and stir. Garnish with the mint sprig.

ROSY CLOVER

SERVES 1

TC: The Clover Club cocktail originated in pre-Prohibition Philadelphia and was named for the club whose members met at the Bellevue-Stratford Hotel in the central part of town. When people outside the club heard about this drink being served to these distinguished gentlemen—viewed as more a Scotch-on-the-rocks type of crowd—they wondered what was so special about this pretty pink concoction that came served in a delicate coupe. What they found was a tart yet well-balanced cocktail with a velvety smooth texture. The drink became suddenly popular but declined not long after. It's thought that the use of raw egg whites gave people pause and a couple of poor write-ups from critics deemed the Clover Club more suitable for the sewing-and-quilting-party crowd. Raspberry syrup was used back in the day, but we're taking advantage of rhubarb season and making our version, the Rosy Clover, with a rhubarb simple syrup instead.

2 oz London dry–style gin

½ oz fresh lemon juice

¾ oz Rhubarb Simple Syrup (page 274)

1 egg white

1 lemon twist

Add the gin, lemon juice, simple syrup, and egg white to a cocktail shaker and dry shake (no ice) for 30 seconds. This allows the egg whites to combine with the other ingredients and create a velvety, foamy texture. Add a handful of ice and shake again for another 30 seconds. Strain into a chilled coupe and garnish with the lemon twist.

WATERMELON SUGAR

SERVES 1

TC: We often associate momentous times in our lives with a favourite song. You'll easily recall your wedding song or what band was popular that summer you first fell in love or the year your baby was born. You'll have a high-school grad song or one that got you through university finals. "Watermelon Sugar" is my 2020–2023 song because I pretty much listened to Harry Styles non-stop. He (and his former bandmates) kept me moving forward, or you could say, in the "one direction" I needed. To honour Mr. Styles, I created this summery cocktail, Watermelon Sugar, named for the catchy track on his album *Fine Line*. This cocktail is pure Harry Styles: good-looking, slightly unconventional, a little sweet, and a little spicy.

Pink sugar, for rim

Flaked salt, for rim

1 lime wedge, for rim

2 cups 2-inch cubed fresh watermelon

½ cup loosely packed whole Thai basil leaves

1½ oz London dry–style gin (see note)

½ oz mellow amaro (see note)

1 tsp chili-infused honey (I use Hive Gourmet's Hive on Fire)

Juice of ½ lime

2 oz rosewater

Mix the sugar and salt in a shallow dish and set aside. Wet the rim of a rocks glass with the lime and dip it into the sugar-salt mix.

Muddle the watermelon with the Thai basil in a cocktail shaker. Add the gin, amaro, honey, lime juice, and rosewater, add ice, and shake for 30 seconds. Add fresh ice to a rocks glass and strain the cocktail into the glass.

NOTE: *Anohka gin, an award-winning London dry-style gin from Alberta, takes the lead as a nod to Harry's UK roots, while Field Notes' Don't Call Me Sweet Pea Garden Amaro, a delicious Alberta spirit made from distilled field peas, is added for balance. An Italian amaro like Montenegro makes a good stand-in if you can't find the Alberta product.*

RHUBARB AMARO SPRITZ

SERVES 1

DC: I am currently on a personal crusade to encourage more folks to use fruit wine in cocktails. There are many, many producers of fruit wine across the Prairies, but my heart will always belong to Saskatchewan's Living Sky Winery. More specifically, their rhubarb wine provides all of those slightly sweet, yet tart vibes one longs for in a nicely chilled rosé on a hot summer's day. This wine spritz is pleasantly spiked with amaro by Saskatoon's Stumbletown Distilling—one of the only distillers producing amaro in the Prairies. It is a drink that's easy to batch, so feel free to make this recipe by the pitcherful and have some friends over for a cheers or two on the back deck!

Honey Rhubarb Simple Syrup

½ cup rhubarb wine (I used Living Sky Winery rhubarb wine)

½ cup unpasteurized honey

Rhubarb Amaro Spritz

4 oz rhubarb wine (I used Living Sky Winery rhubarb wine)

¾ oz good-quality amaro (I used Stumbletown Distilling Mate Amaro)

1 oz honey rhubarb simple syrup

3 oz sparkling water

Honey Rhubarb Simple Syrup

Combine the wine and honey in a small pot and heat over medium heat until the honey has dissolved. Let cool slightly before transferring to a jar or bottle. Store in the fridge until ready to use. Syrup will keep for up to 1 month in a sealed container in the fridge.

Rhubarb Amaro Spritz

Add the wine, amaro, and syrup to a highball glass and stir. Fill with ice and finish with the sparkling water.

FALL

WHAT WE LOVE MOST ABOUT

fall is that while summer adventures may be over, home cooking is back in full force. It's the perfect time of year to make the most of very-much-available produce at the farmers' markets while slowly incorporating comfort foods back into your day-to-day life.

Fall food really kicks into high gear in October. It's full-on sweater weather and there might have even been a snowfall or two, but we're Prairie folks; we're not bothered. Our farmers' markets have squash, carrots, brassicas, and other sturdy vegetables stacked tall and proud, and we'll be damned if we won't take advantage of that. One thing folks do really well in this part of Canada is preserving. We've got to make things last because we know there are even colder, downright frigid, days ahead.

From a beautifully bright squash salad to an indulgent turkey dish, here's how we love to embrace this time of year in the Prairies.

POTATO SALAD WITH HUMMUS HERB DRESSING

SERVES 4–5

DC: A few years back, I went through a big hummus kick. Actually, a *huge* hummus kick. I was not only dunking pitas and crispy veggies into it as a snack, but I also tried many ways to incorporate it into everyday dishes. This potato salad recipe is born of that hummus-centric period of my life, but this time around I am using Twyla's creamy, addictive hemp hummus as a base for the flavourful, herby dressing. Best served on a warm, sunny day in late September so you can pretend that summer hasn't ended after all. Ah, delicious denial.

Hummus Herb Dressing

1½ cups Hemp Hummus (page 141)

⅓ cup finely chopped fresh dill

⅓ cup finely chopped fresh flat-leaf parsley

⅓ cup finely chopped fresh basil

1 Tbsp finely chopped tarragon

2 Tbsp apple cider vinegar

1 Tbsp maple syrup

3–5 Tbsp canola oil

Salt

Potato Salad

20–24 baby potatoes (red, white, or mixed)

1 yellow onion, halved and thinly sliced

4 baby cucumbers, halved and cut into ½-inch slices

12 radishes, tops trimmed and quartered

1 bunch green onions, ends trimmed and coarsely chopped

Hummus Herb Dressing

Place the hummus, dill, parsley, basil, tarragon, vinegar, and maple syrup in a medium bowl and whisk to combine. While whisking, slowly pour in the oil to thin the dressing until it has a pourable consistency. Season to taste with salt and set aside until you are ready to assemble the salad.

Potato Salad

Place the potatoes, onion, cucumber, radishes, and green onions in a large bowl and drizzle ¾ cup of dressing over top. Toss gently until the salad is evenly coated and mixed. Add more dressing if desired.

Leftovers will keep in the fridge for several days, though the cucumbers and radishes will soften notably over time.

NOTE: *Adding an onion when boiling potatoes helps add flavour and also leaves you with tender strips of onion that make a great addition to a potato salad.*

BRAISED LEEKS IN WHEY

MAKES 1½ CUPS

TC: Whey is the tangy by-product that remains once the solids are strained out in the cheesemaking process. Straining dairy products like kefir or yogurt will also reward you with this liquid, which can be used for cooking or baking in place of water, milk, and sometimes even broth. The enzymes in whey help break down fibres in meat, so if you're looking for a no-fuss marinade, whey works wonders. Braising leeks in whey yields a luscious texture, and the flavour develops a rich buttery quality. I like to add a spoonful of these braised leeks on ricotta-topped crostini or mix half a cup into mashed potatoes. They are also the key player in Leeks a' Whey au Gratin (page 82), where they really get to shine in all their luscious glory. If you make our MRKT Fresh Ricotta (page 258), you'll be rewarded with about four cups of whey, but the liquid that comes with store-bought feta or bocconcini is also whey, so you can pilfer that if need be.

3 Tbsp unsalted butter

5 leeks, root end and dark green ends trimmed, sliced into ¼-inch rounds

¼ tsp kosher salt

3 cups whey

In a medium saucepan, melt the butter over medium heat until it's frothy. Add the leeks and salt, and cook until soft, about 10 minutes. Give the mix an occasional stir. Don't let the butter brown, so turn the heat down if necessary.

Add the whey and simmer uncovered until the whey is reduced by half, about 40 minutes. Taste to see if another pinch of salt is needed.

Store in a sealed container in the fridge for up to 2 weeks and warm over low heat before serving. Braised leeks can also be stored in the freezer for up to 6 months.

CRISPY SUNCHOKES WITH HERBED AIOLI

SERVES 4

TC: The first time I made this dish, I knew I was on to something good because I ended up eating the entire batch, snacking on them like French fries. Known by a variety of names—including Jerusalem artichokes and earth apples—sunchokes are neither from Jerusalem nor an artichoke, but rather a species of sunflower. The edible roots look like ginger roots, and while you can eat them raw, they're absolutely dynamite when roasted in the oven. Sunchokes can be harvested at various times of year in Canada but taste best after a hard frost. If the ground remains unfrozen in winter, you can dig these gems up in January. Most often, you'll find them at farmers' markets between November and February. Roasting them until crispy turns these knobby tubers into orbs of glory; great on their own but even better when dipped in an herbed aioli.

2 Tbsp canola oil, divided

1½ lb sunchokes

½ cup Aioli (page 261)

¼ cup chopped fresh flat-leaf parsley

2 Tbsp chopped tarragon

¼ tsp Maldon sea salt, for finishing

Preheat the oven to 425°F. Line a baking sheet with parchment paper and pour 1 Tbsp of the oil over the surface. Use the back of a large spoon to spread the oil evenly on the sheet.

Rinse the sunchokes and cut off any blackened parts. Set a large pot of salted water to boil. Add the sunchokes, cook until fork-tender (about 15 minutes), and drain.

Place the sunchokes on the prepared baking sheet and, with the back of a coffee cup, gently press down on each sunchoke until it cracks and flattens to about ½ inch thick. Drizzle with the remaining 1 Tbsp oil. Bake for 15 minutes, and then turn the sunchokes over with a spatula and bake until they've reached a desirable crispy texture, about 10 minutes more.

While the sunchokes are baking, place the aioli in a small bowl, add the parsley and tarragon, and mix well with a fork.

Finish the sunchokes with Maldon sea salt and serve them warm on a platter with a small bowl of aioli in the centre.

LEEKS A' WHEY AU GRATIN

SERVES 4

TC: If you like French onion soup, you are going to love this hot and cheesy gratin, a dish that uses up a portion of the Braised Leeks in Whey (page 78). This dish will definitely take the chill off frosty autumn days. It's hearty enough to enjoy on its own for lunch, or if you need something more substantial, served with the Brassica (Sort of) Caesar Salad (page 88) or alongside the Alberta Trout Melt (page 100).

1 batch Braised Leeks in Whey
    (page 78; see note)

1 cup chicken or vegetable broth

2 cups Croutons (page 262)

2 cups shredded mozzarella

Preheat the oven to 400°F.

Divide the braised leeks between four French onion soup bowls. You can also put all of the leeks in a small oven-safe casserole dish. Add ¼ cup of broth to each of the four bowls (or 1 cup to the casserole dish) and stir. Top with the croutons, followed by the mozzarella.

Bake for 20 minutes, until browned. If you want a deeper, more bubbly, crust, finish it under the broiler for a couple of minutes.

NOTE: *If the leeks have been frozen, put them in a small saucepan and heat through before putting them into the soup bowls or casserole dish.*

SPICY PICKLED BEETS

MAKES ABOUT 3 PINTS

DC: Just on the outskirts of Saskatoon, you'll find Agar's Corner. The one-part farm, one-part event space plays host to everything from private parties and weddings to drive-in movie nights in the summer. It's also where we hold our annual Prairie Grid Dinner Series when it stops in my hometown of Saskatoon. We've made plenty of memories on the Agars' farm over the years and I look forward to many more. Don and Carmen Agar have shared their simple recipe for spicy pickled beets, and trust me when I say they are *spicy*!

Try using them on a charcuterie board, sliced thin in a turkey sandwich, or even mixed into a traditional beet salad for a little extra kick.

25–30 peeled small beets or 15 peeled large beets, quartered

1½ cups white vinegar

3 Tbsp + 1 tsp salt, divided

¼ tsp minced fresh Carolina Reaper pepper (see note)

1½ cups granulated sugar

½ tsp allspice

⅛ tsp ground cloves

Sterilize eight 16 oz mason jars by removing lids and sealers and placing jars in a large pot with enough water to submerge. Once simmering, allow jars to simmer for 10 minutes.

Use tongs to remove the jars from the pot, pouring out excess water from the jars in the process, and set on the counter until ready to fill.

Place the beets in a large pot or 9-quart Dutch oven and cover with cold water to a depth of 2 inches. Add the vinegar and 3 Tbsp of the salt. Bring to a boil and cook until the beets are tender. Drain the beets, reserving 2 cups of the cooking liquid.

While the beets are cooking, divide the pepper among the sterilized jars. Once the beets are cooled, remove the skins, quarter the beets if you are using large beets, and place them in the jars.

Combine the reserved beet water with the sugar, the remaining 1 tsp salt, and the allspice and cloves and bring to a boil in a medium pot until the sugar has dissolved. Carefully fill the jars with the hot liquid–making sure the beets are fully submerged–and seal the jars, making sure the lids are screwed on tightly.

Bring 2 quarts of water to a simmer in a large deep pot. Working in batches, heat the sealed jars for 5 minutes. Remove the jars from the simmering water and allow them to rest on the counter until they reach room temperature and the tops of jars have popped inward (that is, they are fully sealed).

Once the jars are sealed, you can store the beets in a cool, dry space for up to 2 years. After opening, store in the fridge.

NOTE: *Agar's Corner grows a variety of hot peppers on the farm that they use in all types of pickled goods. If you can't get your hands on a Reaper pepper, a habanero will work too. Let's keep things hot!*

ZUCCHINI RELISH

MAKES 14 CUPS

DC: Now a culinary instructor at the Southern Culinary Institute of Technology, chef Katelin Bland has long been a fixture of the Calgary food scene, working at many top restaurants over the years. In 2019, she joined us on the road for the Prairie Grid Dinner Series, making stunning desserts . . . and a delicious zucchini relish that I couldn't get enough of. This large-batch recipe comes directly from her grandmother's recipe box.

"I grew up with my grandmother's preserves—she always makes the best ones in my opinion. We would always have an excess of zucchini—like everyone who tries to grow it—so she developed this delicious zucchini relish recipe. When she passed it on to me on an old typewritten recipe card that was aged and stained with relish prep splatter, I knew that I had a winner! I love using this on hot dogs or as an accompaniment to a cheese plate." **—Chef Katelin Bland, owner of Katelin's Kitchen**

10 cups grated zucchini

4 cups diced yellow onion

5 Tbsp kosher salt

1 tsp ground turmeric

1 tsp nutmeg

2 tsp celery seed

1 tsp mustard powder

1 Tbsp cornstarch

4 cups granulated sugar

1 green pepper, seeded and diced

1 red pepper, seeded and diced

2 Tbsp diced jalapeño peppers (but feel free to choose the pepper depending on heat strength desired)

2¼ cups white vinegar

Mix the zucchini and onion with the salt. Place in a colander and allow to drain overnight. The next day, rinse the zucchini and onion twice with cold water to remove the salt. Squeeze firmly with clean hands to remove any excess liquid.

Whisk together the turmeric, nutmeg, celery seed, mustard powder, cornstarch, and sugar.

Place all of the dry ingredients plus the zucchini, onions, green pepper, red pepper, jalapeño, and vinegar together in a large stockpot. Mix and bring to a boil over medium heat, stirring often. Allow the relish to boil, uncovered, for 30 minutes. If you prefer a softer consistency, continue to cook for an additional 10–15 minutes.

Once the desired consistency is reached, remove from the heat and allow to cool slightly before transferring to sealable container(s) or jars. The relish will keep in the fridge for up to 2 weeks. If you wish to sterilize and seal jars using a water bath, turn to the recipe on page 84 for instructions.

BRASSICA (SORT OF) CAESAR SALAD

SERVES 4

DC: Most things in the culinary world have been reimagined to the point of exhaustion over the years, and the famed Caesar salad is no exception . . . and now here I am doing the same damn thing! I love the combination of lightly seared brassicas with a beautiful vinaigrette and crunchy croutons. The unexpected presentation of these familiar vegetables will have your dinner guests asking for the recipe after one bite.

Brassicas

2½ cups broccoli florets

2½ cups cauliflower florets

2 Tbsp canola oil, divided

Salt

Apple Cider and Anchovy Vinaigrette

2 Tbsp apple cider vinegar

1 large egg yolk

1 Tbsp anchovy paste

2 tsp Dijon mustard

1 pinch salt

¼ cup canola oil

Assembly

1½ cups Croutons (page 262)

¼ cup finely grated aged Gouda (I use Sylvan Star Cheese Old Grizzly Gouda)

¼ cup thin shavings aged Gouda (I use Sylvan Star Cheese Old Grizzly Gouda)

Brassicas

Bring lightly salted water to a simmer in a large pot over medium-high heat. Working in two batches, blanch the broccoli and cauliflower for 1 minute. Transfer to an ice bath or run under cold tap water to stop the cooking process. Pat until dry with a clean dish towel.

Heat 1 Tbsp of the oil in a large pan on high heat. Once it is very hot, add the broccoli and cook until lightly seared, 3–4 minutes. Transfer the broccoli to a large mixing bowl.

Repeat the process with the remaining 1 Tbsp oil and the cauliflower. Transfer to the same large mixing bowl and season liberally with salt, tossing to coat evenly. Set aside.

Apple Cider and Anchovy Dressing

In a small bowl, whisk together the vinegar, egg yolk, anchovy paste, mustard, and salt. Once combined, slowly pour in the oil while whisking constantly to emulsify. (This process can also be done with a blender.) Set aside until you're ready to assemble the salad. If making this more than an hour or so in advance, keep the dressing in the fridge.

Assembly

Add the croutons, finely grated Gouda, and ⅓ cup of dressing to the mixing bowl with the brassicas and toss to combine. Add more dressing if desired. Transfer to a serving bowl, then top with the thin shavings of Gouda and serve.

ROASTED SQUASH AND HALLOUMI SALAD

SERVES 4

DC: It fills me with much joy to know that locally made halloumi has become more commonplace in the Prairies these past few years. The first time I tried this cheese was when I was in my early twenties and visiting a friend who had just moved across the pond to London. It was love at first bite, and I have held this salty, firm cheese close to my heart ever since. It's this grillable cheese that helps take this squash and apple salad to the next level. My backyard boasts a McIntosh apple tree, so that's what I am using here. If you've got a fruitful tree at your house, feel free to use whatever you're got hanging ripe and ready. Pears work well too!

Fun fact: The grandson of John McIntosh, the man who is credited with discovering the McIntosh sapling and helping commercialize the now-everyday-staple apple in the 1800s, spent the majority of his life in Red Deer, Alberta.

¼ small acorn squash, cut into ½-inch slices (peeled if desired)

½ small butternut squash, peeled and cut into ½-inch slices

8 fresh sage leaves

4 Tbsp canola oil, divided

1 tsp salt

18 oz halloumi, sliced 1 inch long and ½ inch thick (I use Chaeban Artisan Halloumi)

4 cups hand-torn red leaf lettuce

1 McIntosh apple, cored, halved, and thinly sliced

¼ cup salted white pumpkin seeds

½ cup Apple Cider Vinaigrette (page 269)

2 Tbsp maple syrup

Preheat the oven to 400°F. Line a baking sheet with parchment paper.

Place the acorn and butternut squash and the sage leaves in a large bowl. Add 2 Tbsp of the oil and the salt and toss to coat. Transfer to the prepared baking sheet and roast until the squash is tender, 22–25 minutes. Set aside.

Heat the remaining 2 Tbsp of the oil in a large non-stick pan over medium-high heat. Once hot, add the halloumi pieces, leaving space between each. Working in two batches, cook until golden-crispy on both sides, approximately 2 minutes per side. Once cooked, transfer to a paper towel to absorb any excess oil.

Working quickly so the cheese is still served warm, place the squash, lettuce, apple, pumpkin seeds, vinaigrette, and maple syrup in a large bowl. Toss gently to combine. Transfer to a large serving platter or individual plates and top with the halloumi.

BUTTERBALL SOUP

SERVES 6

TC: Butterball (or Butterklösse) soup is a Volga German dish that my mom learned from her mother and is easily one of my favourites. While the recipe could be called "bread dumpling soup," it gets its name for the butter used to both fry and moisten the breadcrumbs. The flavour of those rich bread dumplings infused with warm spices and the comfort that comes with a bowl of noodle soup are a lovely combination.

This recipe is a good example of making a meal out of ingredients that might otherwise go into the garbage bin. The breadcrumbs are made from dry or stale bread, and adding some leftover cooked vegetables to the broth makes the soup more hearty. Traditionally, no vegetables were added, but why not use them up if you've got them? This is a great recipe for kids to help make because rolling the balls is actually quite enjoyable and trying to determine who rolled which balls (based on the size and shape) adds a bit of fun come mealtime. Practise makes perfect when it comes to rolling butterballs, so get those kids and roll!

7½ oz (about 5 slices) dry white bread

7½ oz (about 5 slices) soft white bread

1 tsp salt

1½ Tbsp allspice

1½ tsp nutmeg

5 eggs, lightly beaten

½ cup whole milk, warmed, plus more as needed

½ cup butter

1 cup long pasta broken into small pieces

6 cups chicken broth

In the bowl of a food processor, add the pieces of dry bread and pulse until the breadcrumbs are fine. Transfer the breadcrumbs to a large bowl. Repeat the process with the fresh bread and leave those breadcrumbs in the food processor to be used later.

In a large bowl, mix the dry breadcrumbs with the salt, allspice, and nutmeg. Add the lightly beaten eggs and milk. Stir to mix well.

Melt the butter in a deep frying pan and add the fresh breadcrumbs. Stir constantly to make sure they don't burn. When they are golden brown, add them to the breadcrumb-egg-milk mixture, and stir until everything is combined.

Fill a large pot with water on the stove and heat to boiling.

continued on next page

When forming the balls, aim for a size close to that of a ping-pong ball. (They will expand a bit when cooked.) Gently squeeze the moistened crumbs by scrunching the portion in one hand to compact the crumbs and then roll it into a ball using both hands. The butterball should be smooth and well compacted. If the mixture doesn't hold, add a bit more milk to the breadcrumb mixture, mix well, and try rolling a ball again. Drop one ball into a pot of boiling water. If it holds together, you're good to go.

In a separate pot, bring water to boil and cook pasta according to the package instructions. Set aside. (You'll add this pasta to your chicken broth after the butterballs are cooked.)

Bring the chicken broth in a separate pot to a gentle boil and drop in the number of butterballs you need for your meal. People usually eat three or four dumplings each. Butterballs are done when they float to the top.

Add the pasta to the soup bowls, top each with 4 butterballs, and add the broth. Leftover butterball soup can be stored in a lidded container in the fridge for up to 4 days, but the texture of both the dumplings and the pasta will become flabby from soaking up the broth. It's best to eat this dish as soon as it's made.

COLOUR: *Butterballs will vary in colour with every batch you make depending on how deeply the breadcrumbs brown in the pan and depending on the type of bread used. The recipe calls for white bread, but you can use other types, like a light rye or whole wheat bread, if you have other breads you don't want to throw out. Avoid ancient grain or heavily seeded breads, as those larger grains and seeds will make the balls fall apart.*

FLAVOUR: *Allspice is vital to this dish. Add more or less, depending on how much you like it.*

TECHNIQUE: *This is one of those recipes where you get better with every batch you make. Just like perogies, where your pinching technique gets better the more you pinch, your rolling technique will improve the more balls you make. If the ball falls apart when you try to roll it, that means you haven't compacted it enough.*

YIELD: *The number of butterballs you end up with depends on how big you make them, but you can count on getting about four dozen balls out of this recipe. To serve six, count on four butterballs each. The remaining balls can be stored in the freezer for up to 2 months. To freeze, place the balls on a parchment-lined baking sheet in the freezer and transfer to a bag or lidded container once frozen. To cook from frozen, place the balls in the hot broth and simmer. They are done when they float to the surface, about 10 minutes, or when a toothpick is easily inserted into the centre.*

FALL FAGIOLI SOUP

SERVES 4–6

DC: I love making a big batch of soup when the first fall cold snap hits. Filled to the brim with Prairie-grown ingredients like lentils, beans, wild rice, and earthy parsnips and beet greens, this warming soup will leave you wanting for nothing after a few sips.

2 Tbsp sunflower oil

2 yellow onions, diced

1 Tbsp butter or vegan butter

1 clove garlic, minced

5 cups vegetable broth

1 cup water

1 cup peeled and diced parsnips

½ cup dried red split lentils

1 can (14 oz) kidney beans, plus half the can liquid

1 tsp coarsely chopped fresh oregano

1 tsp dried basil

⅓ cup wild rice (I like Northern Lights Foods organic brand)

Salt

2 tsp apple cider vinegar

4 cups coarsely chopped beet greens

Toasted bread of choice, for serving (optional)

Heat the oil in a large pot over medium-high heat. Add the onions and cook for 10 minutes, stirring occasionally, until the onions begin to turn golden. (If brown bits form on the bottom of the pot, add small splashes of water to help deglaze it.) Reduce the heat to medium, add the butter and garlic, and continue to cook for 5 minutes, stirring occasionally.

Next, add the broth, water, parsnips, lentils, kidney beans (plus reserved can liquid), oregano, basil, and rice. Once the mixture comes to a simmer, cook uncovered for 20 minutes. The soup should thicken slightly.

Season to taste with salt. Add the vinegar and beet greens and continue to cook for 5 minutes to allow the greens to become tender. Serve with toasted bread.

BUTTERNUT SQUASH, CARROT, AND PARMESAN SOUP

SERVES 4-5

DC: It's not fall unless you eat your fair share of butternut squash soup, am I right? One of the things that I love most about this time of year is seeing the sky-high mounds of squash at local farmers' markets and grocers. With this soup recipe, you'll find all of the comforting flavours of fall in one bowl. I love combining squash and carrots for their subtle sweetness, but also for their perfectly cozy colour when cooked and blended together.

1 Tbsp canola oil

1 yellow onion, diced

3 cloves garlic, minced

1 Tbsp butter

½ cup dry white wine

3 cups peeled, diced butternut squash

2 cups diced carrots (peeled if desired)

6 cups vegetable broth

1 tsp finely chopped fresh oregano

1 tsp finely chopped fresh rosemary

2 cups half and half cream

½ cup freshly grated parmesan

1 Tbsp apple cider vinegar

Salt

Chopped fresh flat-leaf parsley, for garnish (optional)

Heat the oil in a large pot on medium-high heat. Once hot, add the onion and garlic and cook until softened and fragrant, 2–3 minutes. Add the butter and continue to cook, stirring often, for several more minutes. Next, add the wine, squash, and carrots to the pot and continue to cook, stirring occasionally, until the wine reduces by half, about 5 minutes. Add the broth, oregano, and rosemary to the pot and bring to a simmer over medium-low heat. Reduce to medium heat and allow to cook until the carrots and squash are fork-tender.

Using an immersion blender, purée the soup until very smooth. Stir in the cream and parmesan and cook for another 10 minutes, stirring occasionally.

Add the vinegar, season to taste with salt, and keep warm on the stove until ready to serve. Garnish with parsley when serving.

ALBERTA TROUT MELT

SERVES 4

DC: As a kid, I had an unabashed love of tuna sandwiches. When I grew older and my tastes evolved, I fell head over heels for tuna *melts* . . . likely because of the addition of slightly broiled, gooey cheese on top of a dish I already looked forward to devouring. Plus, now that it's a little cooler out, a plate of food like this is wonderful to cozy up to. It's as fun to elevate a classic melt as it is rewarding. Use a good-quality cut of lake trout and your favourite locally made sourdough as a toasty base, and this recipe will not lead you astray.

Pan-Cooked Trout

2 Tbsp canola oil, divided

2 cloves garlic, minced

2 shallots, diced

½ tsp salt

1 side of trout, skin on, bones removed, halved lengthwise

2 Tbsp pickle brine

Pickle Aioli

3 Tbsp mayonnaise

1 Tbsp grainy Dijon mustard

¼ cup diced garlic dill pickles

¼ cup diced celery

1 Tbsp canola oil

1 Tbsp pickle brine

Assembly

4–6 slices sourdough bread, approximately 1 inch thick

Mayonnaise

1 cup freshly shredded 2-year-old cheddar

Pan-Cooked Trout

Heat 1 Tbsp of oil in a medium pan over medium-high heat for 1 minute. Add the garlic and shallots and cook until softened, 2–3 minutes. Transfer to a medium mixing bowl, season with the salt, and set aside.

Add the remaining 1 Tbsp oil to the pan. Once hot, add the trout fillets, skin down, and cook for 5 minutes. Flip over and, while the trout continues to cook, gently remove and discard the skin by pulling it away from the flesh with tongs. Add the brine and use tongs to break up the trout meat into bite-sized chunks. Once cooked through, 3–4 minutes, combine with the shallot mixture and let cool in the fridge for 15 minutes to help return the mixture to room temperature before assembling.

Pickle Aioli

Place the mayonnaise, mustard, pickles, celery, oil, and brine in a small mixing bowl and stir well to combine.

Assembly

Preheat the oven to 375°F.

Slather the slices of sourdough bread with mayonnaise and place the bread on a baking sheet. Spoon even portions of the trout mixture onto each slice of sourdough and top generously with the cheese.

Bake for 8–10 minutes or until the cheese has noticeably melted. Finish by broiling for 2 minutes to allow the cheese to bubble and brown. Remove from the oven and allow to cool slightly before serving.

NOTE: *Both the trout and aioli can be made a day or two before assembly if desired.*

STIR-FRIED TOMATO AND EGG
SERVES 2

DC: Carmen Cheng's family recipe for a tomato and egg dish can be made year-round but tastes especially fantastic while tomatoes are still in season. If we're lucky, that means we can enjoy this dish to its fullest until middle to late October.

This stir-fried tomato and egg dish was common on our dinner table, or for a quick lunch. During the beginning of the pandemic, I was seeking comfort foods from my childhood and shared this dish on Instagram. It warmed my heart how many messages I received from others whose families also used to make this dish. Every family has their own version—this is the one from my childhood."—**Carmen Cheng, Calgary-based food writer**

2 Tbsp sunflower or canola oil, divided

2 large eggs, 1 beaten, 1 whole

1 clove garlic, smashed and left whole

2–3 large Roma tomatoes, quartered

Salt

1 Tbsp ketchup, plus more for seasoning

Cooked rice, for serving

Heat ½ Tbsp of the oil in a medium pan and scramble 1 egg over medium heat. Transfer to a bowl and set aside.

Using the same pan, reduce the heat to low, and add the garlic and the remaining 1½ Tbsp oil. Gently cook for 1–2 minutes to infuse the garlic in the oil. Add the tomatoes and a pinch of salt. Put a lid on the pan and turn the heat up to medium-low. Let this cook for a few minutes until the tomatoes have softened and are starting to break down. Remove the lid and discard the clove garlic. Add the ketchup to the pan, stir, and let the mixture cook for another minute or so to continue to soften.

Crack the second egg into the tomato mixture and stir frequently. This will help thicken the tomato mixture within 1 minute to a scrambled egg–like consistency. Once thickened, turn the heat to low and return the scrambled egg to the pan, stirring gently to combine.

Taste for seasoning, adding salt or ketchup as needed. Serve over rice and enjoy.

NOTE: *Carmen says, "Many families have their own variation of this dish. Popular add-ins include onions, green onions, sliced beef, ginger, fish sauce, and sugar (instead of ketchup)."*

PEAR AND BRIE TARTS WITH ROASTED SHALLOTS AND GARLIC

MAKES 18 TARTS

TC: The filling in these two-bite tarts couldn't be easier: just add fresh pears to our Roasted Shallots and Garlic (page 257). Pop in a cube of cheese to melt as the tart bakes, finish with crushed pink peppercorns to balance the dish, and you've got a luscious little number that will bring the wow factor to any table. Serve with a dark beer or an earthy wine like a pinot noir.

Pear Jam

½ cup Roasted Shallots and Garlic (page 257), drained of oil

2 ripe pears, peeled and cut into chunks

3 Tbsp turbinado sugar

2 tsp apple cider vinegar

Assembly

18 mini frozen pastry tart shells (each 2 inches) (remove from freezer 10 minutes before needed) (see note)

4 oz brie cheese, ½-inch cubes (about 1 cup)

1 Tbsp pink peppercorns, crushed

NOTE: *Look for tart shells that come in foil shells to help the tarts keep their shape while baking.*

Preheat the oven to 385°F and line a baking sheet with parchment paper.

Pear Jam

Add the shallots and garlic, plus the pears, sugar, and vinegar, to a small saucepan and bring to a gentle boil. Turn the heat to low and gently simmer for 15 minutes or until the pears have broken down and the mixture has thickened. Remove and discard any residual oil that is sitting on top by pressing a soup spoon gently on top of the mixture, then tipping the saucepan so it runs out.

Assembly

Arrange the mini tart shells on the prepared baking sheet and fill with 1 Tbsp of pear jam. Top with 2 small cubes of cheese, pushing them slightly into the jam.

Bake for 15 minutes or until the jam is bubbling, the cheese has melted, and the pastry is golden brown. If needed, rotate the tray and set the timer for 5 more minutes. Remove and sprinkle with the crushed peppercorns. Remove the tarts from their foil shells before placing on a tray to serve. Allow the tarts to cool for 10 minutes before eating.

The tarts can be kept in a sealed container in the fridge for up to 1 week, and reheated in a 300°F oven for 10 minutes (or a microwave on medium power for a minute) before serving.

FARINATA WITH MUSHROOMS AND PECORINO CHEESE

SERVES 2-4

TC: This is a recipe adapted from chef Becky Ross, when she owned the Camp Cookhouse in Elkwater, a community in southern Alberta. I have dreamed of this dish since I first tasted it at the restaurant several years ago. Farinata (in Italy) or socca (in France) is a chickpea pancake, commonly served as street food. Farinata is highly customizable. Don't like cumin? Try crushed fennel instead. Top it with roasted vegetables if you're not into mushrooms, or don't top it with anything at all. As for cheese, any hard cheese that you can grate is fine. A spritz of lemon juice at the end brings all the best features of this little pancake to the forefront. Both the batter and the mushroom mix can be made a day ahead; just make sure to remix the batter before putting it into the pan, and gently reheat the mushrooms before the final assembly. The process may look exhausting, but it's not—I would use the word "detailed," but it will only take you one time to realize this dish will be in your culinary repertoire forever.

Farinata

⅔ cup chickpea flour

¾ cup water

½ tsp salt

1 pinch ground cumin

1 pinch ground coriander

½ tsp finely chopped fresh thyme or finely crushed dried thyme

1 very small clove of garlic, finely grated

½ cup pecorino cheese, grated

Mushroom Topping

2 Tbsp canola oil, divided

1 Tbsp butter

2 cups mixed mushrooms (a blend of cremini, shiitake, and oyster works well)

Farinata

Place the chickpea flour in a bowl and slowly add the water, whisking as you add it. You want to make a smooth paste first, then slowly thin it. Use an immersion blender if you run into trouble. Add the salt, cumin, coriander, thyme, garlic, and cheese and mix. Allow the mixture to sit for at least 30 minutes.

Mushroom Topping

While the farinata batter is resting, add 1 Tbsp of oil and the butter to a medium sauté pan and heat over medium heat. Once the butter has melted, add the mushrooms, stir, and fry for 10 minutes or until golden. Add a pinch of salt to taste, and set aside.

In a small pan, heat the remaining 1 Tbsp oil over medium heat, add the shallot, and cook until translucent. Turn the heat to medium-low, and after about 30 seconds add the garlic and

continued on next page

Salt

1 medium shallot or ½ small onion, thinly sliced

3 cloves garlic, thinly sliced

Freshly cracked black pepper

½ tsp finely chopped fresh thyme

½ tsp finely chopped fresh sage

Assembly

2 Tbsp canola oil

½ cup pecorino cheese, grated

½ cup coarsely chopped fresh flat-leaf parsley

½ lemon, cut into 4 wedges

a pinch or two of salt, stirring often until the garlic is cooked through and both the shallot and garlic are a pale gold colour. Add the pepper, thyme, and sage, stir to combine, and remove from the heat. Add this mixture to the mushrooms and toss to combine. Set aside.

Assembly

Preheat the oven to 500°F.

Once the batter has sat, and your mushrooms are ready, put a medium oven-safe pan over medium-high heat and allow it to get fully hot. Add the canola oil and gently swirl in the pan to ensure the pan is coated up the sides. Pour the farinata batter into the pan.

After a few seconds, when the edges start to set up, take your spatula and try to run it along the edges of the pancake, coaxing the oil that has risen to the top of the batter down the sides and underneath the pancake. Try to gently slide the spatula underneath the whole pancake.

Place the pan in the oven for about 5 minutes, or until the batter is no longer runny. Remove the pan from the oven and use the spatula to help flip the pancake. Pile your mushroom mixture onto the top of the pancake and pop it back into the oven to roast until the mushrooms are heated through, about 5 minutes more.

Remove the pan from the oven, place on a trivet, and garnish with cheese and parsley. Serve with lemon wedges and eat the farinata warm or at room temperature.

ROSEMARY POTATO "RISOTTO"
WITH ROAST TURKEY BREAST

SERVES 4

DC: Potato risotto is just a fancy way of saying you cooked little cubes of potato in a rich, creamy broth. By opting to slowly simmer the potatoes in this way, you wind up with a delicious end product reminiscent of a turkey dinner! If the pandemic taught us anything, it's that having a holiday dinner for simply two or four is just as rewarding as a whole extended family affair. In that vein, this is a perfect recipe for those of you who prefer smaller gatherings sans in-laws, cousins, and whoever else adds to the seat count and may stress you out. A bone-in turkey breast yields a lot more meat than you might think at first glance. When it's finished roasting and the meat has been sliced, it is easily portionable into four servings.

Roast Turkey Breast

2 Tbsp butter, at room temperature

1 bone-in turkey breast (2–2½ lb)
    (see note)

1 yellow onion, thinly sliced

2 Tbsp water

1 Tbsp canola oil

½ tsp salt

Rosemary Potato "Risotto"

1 Tbsp canola oil

1 yellow onion, diced

2 cloves garlic, minced

1 Tbsp butter

4 cups red potatoes, diced

1 tsp dried rosemary

1¼ cups turkey or chicken broth

¼ cup half and half cream

¼ cup finely grated aged Gouda
    (I use Sylvan Star Cheese Old
    Grizzly Gouda)

Salt

Roast Turkey Breast

Preheat the oven to 375°F.

Using your hands, distribute the butter evenly under the skin of the turkey breast.

In a small baking dish, combine the onion, water, and oil. Nestle the turkey breast on top, sprinkle the salt evenly across everything, and cover loosely with tinfoil.

Roast until the internal temperature registers between 145°F and 150°F, about 45 minutes. Remove the tinfoil and roast uncovered to help the skin crisp up until the temperature rises to 165°F, about 15 minutes more. Let rest, covered, while you prepare the remaining components.

Rosemary Potato "Risotto"

Heat the oil in a medium sauté pan over medium-high heat. Add the onion and garlic and cook for 5 minutes, stirring occasionally, to allow the onions to become translucent and notably softened. Add the butter, stir, and continue to cook for another 5 minutes or until the onions begin to turn golden.

continued on next page

Fried Sage

¼ cup canola oil

12 fresh sage leaves

Assembly

¼ cup dry breadcrumbs

¼ tsp freshly ground black pepper

1 pinch dried sage

1 pinch dried thyme

Add the potatoes, rosemary, and broth. Once the mixture begins to simmer, reduce the heat to medium and continue to cook until the potatoes are al dente (slightly firm in the middle), about 10 minutes.

Add the cream and Gouda to the pan and continue to cook for another 5–7 minutes, until the liquid has thickened noticeably and the potatoes are tender. Season to taste with salt, reduce the heat to low, and keep warm until ready to serve.

Fried Sage

Heat the oil in a small pan over medium-high heat. Once the oil is hot, add the sage and let them pan fry until they turn a deep forest green, 30–45 seconds. Transfer to a paper towel to absorb any excess oil and let cool.

Assembly

In a small bowl, mix together the breadcrumbs, pepper, sage, and thyme, stirring to combine.

Divide the potato "risotto" evenly between four bowls, top with the turkey and the breadcrumb mixture, and garnish with the fried sage.

NOTE: *Don't forget to save the bones and make a mini batch of turkey broth too. Talk about killing two birds with one stone!*

SLOW-COOKED WHITE BEANS WITH HAM HOCK AND HOMEMADE BARBECUE SAUCE

SERVES 4

TC: Having grown up in Saskatchewan, Vancouver chef Dawn Doucette has a deep love of the Prairies, returning to visit her family every summer. One of her favourite food memories of Saskatchewan is of the slow-cooked beans that her grandmother, Irene, made. This dish was a mainstay during many family dinners over the years. Nowadays, the beans have found a home on the menu at her wildly popular a.m. eatery, Douce Diner. The tender beans have become a signature dish here, perfectly complemented by her homemade barbecue sauce.

"The braised white beans were often on my grandmother's table for dinner, and lunch the next day would see the warmed beans spread on homemade toasted bread that was slathered in mayo." —**Dawn Doucette, chef at Douce Diner**

Barbecue Sauce (makes 1 quart)

2 tsp fennel seed

2½ tsp cumin seed

1 Tbsp coriander seed

2 tsp celery seed

1¼ tsp mustard seed

2 tsp black peppercorns

2 Tbsp canola oil

3 white onions, grated

3 cloves garlic, peeled and grated

½ cup apple juice

½ cup apple cider vinegar

½ cup + 2 Tbsp maple syrup

½ cup yellow mustard (I use French's)

½ cup blackstrap molasses

5 Tbsp apricot preserves

1¾ cups ketchup

2 oz chipotle peppers

2 Tbsp smoked Maldon sea salt

Barbecue Sauce

Toast the fennel seed, cumin seed, coriander seed, celery seed, mustard seed, and peppercorns in a medium-sized dry pan over medium heat for a few minutes, shaking the pan until the seeds turn golden. Transfer to a shallow dish and allow to cool. Place the toasted spices in a food processor and blitz to a coarse powder.

Heat the oil over medium heat in a medium heavy-bottomed pot. Add the onions, garlic, and ground spice mixture and cook for about 10 minutes or until the onions are cooked through. (This is important because undercooked onions will taint the finished sauce with an unpleasant raw onion flavour.)

Add the apple juice and vinegar and bring to a simmer until reduced by one-third. Add the maple syrup, mustard, molasses, preserves, ketchup, chipotles, and smoked sea salt, bring to a simmer, and continue to simmer for about 5 minutes.

continued on next page

Braised White Beans

2 lb dried white navy beans

1 white onion (about 5 oz), quartered

1 smoked ham hock, about 2½ lb

10 cups cold water (or enough to cover the hock)

1 Tbsp + 2 tsp kosher salt

6 Tbsp apple cider vinegar

Purée the sauce with either a hand-held immersion blender or in a standing blender until the mixture is smooth. Pass the sauce through a fine-mesh sieve. Store in a sealed container in the fridge for up to 2 weeks.

Braised White Beans

Preheat the oven to 350°F.

Rinse the beans under cold water until the water runs clear (see note).

Place the beans, onion, ham hock, 1 Tbsp of the kosher salt, and water in a large (9-quart) Dutch oven and cover with a securely fitting lid. Bake for 3 hours without stirring. Add more hot water and cook longer if required to make the beans al dente. Once removed from the oven, allow to cool slightly. Do not drain.

Remove the ham hock from the beans. Shred all of the meat, discarding the bone, gristle, skin, and fat, and place the shredded meat back into the beans. Add the remaining 2 tsp kosher salt and the vinegar, adjusting to taste, and stir gently to combine.

Serve the beans with the barbecue sauce on the side. Leftover beans can be stored in a sealed container in the fridge for up to 4 days.

NOTE: *Dawn doesn't soak the beans overnight. Rather, she simply rinses them in cold water until the water runs clear, removing any grit or bad beans. Be sure to check the beans halfway through the cooking time, and if they are still hard, add more water as needed. It's important to not strain the beans when they're done, as you will want to retain the liquid. If you prefer to soak the beans overnight, use the same recipe but cook the beans for about 1 hour.*

SPATCHCOCKED PAPRIKA CHICKEN WITH SAVOY CABBAGE AND CARROTS

SERVES 6

TC: This is a beautiful sheet-pan meal that appears more complicated than it is. A spatchcocked bird has the backbone removed so that the bird lies flat. This allows the bird to cook evenly and in a relatively short time. Placing the chicken on top of the vegetables allows the vegetables to baste and cook in the juices as the bird roasts. While we use Savoy cabbage and carrots for this early fall dish, switching them out for root vegetables, like parsnips and Brussels sprouts, makes this enjoyable in late fall or winter as well. The seasoning spices are adjustable, but this blend is paprika forward and inspired by a dish my mom used to make.

Spice Blend

1 Tbsp mild Hungarian paprika

1 tsp salt

1 tsp garlic powder

1 tsp onion powder

½ tsp black pepper

1 tsp crushed coriander seed
(see note)

2 Tbsp canola oil, divided

1 medium Savoy cabbage, cut into
1-inch-thick slabs

4 unpeeled carrots, sliced in half
lengthwise

1 tsp salt

½ tsp freshly ground black pepper

1 roasting chicken (4 lb)

2 tsp flaky sea salt

1 lemon, cut into 8 pieces

Preheat the oven to 425°F.

Spice Blend

Combine the paprika, salt, garlic powder, onion powder, pepper, and coriander in a small bowl. Set aside.

Drizzle 1 Tbsp of the oil on a large baking sheet or shallow roasting pan (18 × 13 × 2 inches), making sure it's coated, then lay down the cabbage and carrots and sprinkle with salt and pepper.

To spatchcock the chicken, place the chicken, breast side down, on a cutting board and with kitchen shears cut up along one side of the backbone, starting at the tail and working your way up to the neck. Repeat the process on the other side of the backbone. Save that backbone for broth by placing it in a ziplock bag in the freezer. Flip the bird over and press down on the breast to flatten.

Rub the chicken with the remaining 1 Tbsp oil and cover it with the spice blend. Put the chicken on top of the vegetables and place the baking sheet in the oven.

continued on next page

Roast for about 50 minutes or until the internal temperature reaches 165°F. The skin should be golden brown and crispy and juice from the thigh, when pierced with a fork, should run clear. Let rest for 10 minutes.

Place the pan in the centre of the table, on top of a wooden cutting board or metal trivets. Finish the bird with a scatter of flaky sea salt. Serve the lemon on the side, to spritz on the chicken after pieces are cut and served.

NOTE: *To crush seeds, I use a mortar and pestle, but if you don't have one, place the coriander seeds on a cutting board and use the flat side of a large knife to crush them.*

DILL PICKLE–BRINED PORK TENDERLOIN

SERVES 3–4

DC: My love for pickled vegetable brine runs deep. So deep, in fact, that I love using it to make cuts of meat taste even more delicious. Here's a great way to put my sentiments into action that results in a delicious main affair for the dinner table.

2 cups good-quality pickle brine (most standard jars of pickles will yield about 2 cups of brine)

1 yellow onion, halved and thinly sliced

16–18 oz pork tenderloin

1 Tbsp canola oil

1 Tbsp water

1 batch glaze from Mustard and Brown Sugar–Glazed Meatloaf (page 175)

Combine the pickle brine, onion, and tenderloin in a large zip-lock bag or a shallow bowl (covered) and let sit in the fridge for a minimum of 8 hours, up to 24 hours maximum. (This step is easily done the night before or in the morning.)

When ready to cook, strain and discard the brine from the pork and onions. Let the mixture rest at room temperature for 20 minutes.

Preheat the oven to 400°F.

In a medium baking dish, combine the oil, water, and brined onions to create an even bottom layer. Nestle the pork on top of the onions and brush with the glaze until nicely coated.

Roast for 25 minutes, glazing the pork twice more during this time, until the pork registers an internal temperature of 150°F. The pork will brown notably as well.

Transfer the pork to a cutting board and cover with tinfoil to rest for 10 minutes. The pork's internal temperature should continue to rise, and reach 160°F after several minutes. Slice and return the pork to rest on top of the cooked onions in the baking dish for serving.

NOTE: *If you've got a favourite glaze or barbecue sauce, feel free to use it instead of our mustard sauce. The pickle brine is the important factor here.*

BRAISED BEEF TONGUE

TC: It's no mystery why certain parts of the animal often get overlooked, especially when those parts are referred to as "offal." The term actually comes from "off fall," as in the parts cast off the table during butchery—things like organs and extremities (think brains and tails). But if you're on board with the idea of whole-animal butchery and nose-to-tail eating, then all those extra parts that may not sound appetizing, like tongue, for instance, should find their way into your cooking repertoire.

The key to working with this cut is boiling the tongue for a few hours first and then peeling off the outer layer of skin. After that, it's smooth sailing into a ridiculously succulent and deeply delicious dining experience. I think cooked tongue is best when it's finished simply with a flaky sea salt and eaten warm, but if you have leftovers, it makes a dynamite stroganoff too (see Beef Tongue Stroganoff, page 123).

1 beef tongue (about 3 lb)

1 large white or yellow onion, quartered

2 large carrots, chopped

2 celery stalks, chopped

2 cloves garlic

1 sprig fresh rosemary

2 sprigs fresh thyme

2 bay leaves

2 tsp black or mixed peppercorns

¼ tsp Maldon sea salt

Freshly cracked black pepper

Relish or creamed horseradish

Rinse the tongue well, place it in a large stockpot, and add the onion, carrots, celery, garlic, rosemary, thyme, bay leaves, and peppercorns, plus enough water to cover the tongue by 1 inch. Bring to a boil, turn the heat to low, cover, and simmer for 3 hours.

Prepare an ice bath in a large bowl. When the cooking time is up, remove the tongue with tongs and place it in the cold water to chill just enough that you can easily handle it with your hands. Don't pour out the braising liquid–strain it and freeze it in a sealable container to use in any recipe that calls for beef broth.

Place the tip of a sharp knife under the skin at the back of the tongue and use it to just lift the skin. From there, you can easily peel the skin off in strips. Discard the skin and use the knife to trim off any gristle or extra fat.

The ways to enjoy cooked tongue are endless. Season with salt and pepper, drizzle some braising liquid over the sliced meat and eat it warm with a condiment like relish or creamed horseradish. Cooled beef tongue is lovely as a sandwich meat.

BEEF TONGUE STROGANOFF

SERVES 4

TC: Stroganoff is a dish with mid-nineteenth-century Russian roots. It is named for a member of the Stroganovs, an influential family at the time. Mushrooms didn't feature in the original recipe but are commonly added these days, as they were back in the 1970s when I first learned how to make this dish from my mom. She used leftover beef roast, which drastically shortened the preparation time and also helped prevent food waste. Leftover Braised Beef Tongue (page 120) is perfect for this dish because of how tender it is. Serve this saucy stroganoff over noodles, and you can have dinner on the table in well under an hour.

2 Tbsp canola oil

2 Tbsp butter

3 cups cremini mushrooms, quartered

¾ cup white or yellow onion, diced

¼ cup white wine

2 cups cubed Braised Beef Tongue (page 120)

1½ Tbsp all-purpose flour

1½ cups beef broth

2 sprigs fresh thyme

½ tsp salt

⅛ tsp black pepper

¼ cup sour cream

1½ tsp Dijon mustard

To a medium (5-quart) Dutch oven set over medium-high heat, add the oil and butter and heat until melted.

Add the mushrooms and sauté for a few minutes until golden, stirring often to prevent burning. Turn the heat to medium, add the onion, and stir and sauté until softened, about 4 minutes.

Add the wine to deglaze the pan, using a wooden spoon to stir and scrape up the browned bits. When the wine has reduced by half, add the beef, stir a few times, and then sprinkle the flour overtop. Stir to ensure the pieces are evenly coated. Add the broth, thyme, salt, and pepper, stir to combine all the ingredients, and turn the heat to medium-low. Simmer for 10 minutes. Stir in the sour cream and let cook for a minute more.

Add the mustard just before the dish is ready to be plated. Serve over egg noodles. Store leftover stroganoff in a sealed container in the fridge for up to 1 week.

THREE SISTERS SPICE COOKIES

MAKES 24 COOKIES

DC: One of the most noteworthy chefs in Saskatchewan is, without a doubt, Jenni Lessard. Jenni is Métis, and her leadership in the Indigenous culinary community has helped bring life to many impactful culinary events, including the Han Wi Moon dinner experiences at Wanuskewin. Perhaps most importantly, Jenni has worked with the Saskatchewan Health Authority to create a one-of-a-kind Indigenous-specific hospital food program for Saskatoon hospital patients. This cookie recipe was developed for the hospital program and presents an iconic trifecta of Indigenous ingredients.

"These soft and moist cookies pay homage to the time-honoured Indigenous companion planting method using corn, bean, and squash." —Chef Jenni Lessard, owner of Inspired by Nature Culinary Consulting

Cinnamon Sugar Coating

1 cup granulated sugar

1 tsp cinnamon

Cookies

½ cup soft vegan margarine or sunflower oil

½ cup granulated sugar

½ cup packed brown sugar

1½ cups cooked butternut squash purée (see note)

1 tsp vanilla

1 cup all-purpose flour

1 cup whole wheat flour

½ cup cornmeal

1 tsp baking soda

1 tsp baking powder

1 tsp cinnamon

½ tsp ground ginger

½ tsp salt

Cinnamon Sugar Coating

Combine the sugar and cinnamon in a small bowl and set aside until the cookie dough is ready to be portioned out.

Cookies

Preheat the oven to 350°F. Line a baking sheet with parchment paper.

Combine the margarine, granulated sugar, brown sugar, squash purée, and vanilla in a medium bowl and beat with an electric mixer until light and creamy.

Mix together the all-purpose flour, whole wheat flour, cornmeal, baking soda, baking powder, cinnamon, ginger, and salt in a large bowl. Add the wet ingredients and the black beans to the dry ingredients. Stir well to combine.

Scoop the dough by the tablespoonful, roll into a ball, and roll in a bowl with the cinnamon sugar mixture until coated. Flatten each ball between your palms and place it on the prepared baking sheet.

1 cup cooked black beans, rinsed and coarsely chopped

Bake for about 12 minutes, until lightly browned around the edges. Transfer to a cooling rack and let the cookies sit for 15 minutes before transferring to a sealed container. The other option? Devour immediately.

NOTES: *1. These are vegan and can be made gluten-free by substituting the flour with an equal amount of gluten-free flour. 2. Cook peeled and diced butternut squash in a medium pot with just enough water to cover it, until easily pierced with a fork, about 12–14 minutes. Then drain and purée in a blender or food processor. Substitute canned pumpkin if you don't have squash.*

HEMP AND SASKATOON BERRY GRANOLA BARS

MAKES 2 DOZEN GRANOLA BARS

DC: I don't have kids running around my home, so I don't feel the energy of back-to-school season like a lot of folks do, but what I do feel is a renewed interest in granola bars come September. These granola bars are the perfect healthy-ish snack for kids or kids at heart (like me) and don't take long to make. I love the chew of dried Saskatoon berries in this recipe, but feel free to swap them out for other dried fruit such as dried cherries, blueberries, or cranberries.

¾ cup maple syrup

⅓ cup sunflower seed butter

2 Tbsp unpasteurized honey

2 Tbsp butter

½ tsp salt

3 large egg whites, whisked until foamy

4 cups quick oats

½ cup hemp hearts

½ cup salted pumpkin seeds

1 cup dried Saskatoon berries

1 tsp ground pumpkin pie spice blend

Preheat the oven to 350°F. Line a 9 × 13-inch cake pan with parchment paper.

Heat the maple syrup, sunflower seed butter, honey, butter, and salt in a small pot over medium heat, stirring occasionally. Once melted together, remove from the heat.

Place the foamy egg whites, oats, hemp hearts, pumpkin seeds, Saskatoon berries, and pumpkin pie spice in a large mixing bowl and mix to combine. Pour the maple syrup mixture over top and stir until the dry ingredients are uniformly coated.

Transfer to the prepared baking tray and press down the granola mixture until it evenly covers the whole tray.

Bake for 20 minutes or until lightly golden. Remove and let cool completely before slicing into bars. Store in a sealable container in the fridge or at room temperature for up to 1 week. The bars can be wrapped individually and frozen as well.

NOTE: *To keep things vegan here, you can use plant-based butter, then skip the egg whites, and still end up with a tasty finished product. It will be much softer though, so I would recommend freezing the tray once it's finished baking before slicing into individual bars.*

SPICED COFFEE CAKE

TC: Coffee cakes date back to seventeenth-century north and central Europe where sweet Viennese-style offerings were eaten with coffee or tea in the afternoons. This style of cake is believed to have been brought to the Americas by German immigrants, but no matter its origin, this cake, laden with warm spices, evokes all that is autumn to me: the weight of September sunshine, the colours of leaves changing from green to gold, the long days of harvest, and the anticipation of Thanksgiving dinner.

2 cups all-purpose flour

1 tsp baking soda

1 tsp cinnamon

1 tsp ground cloves

1 tsp allspice

1 tsp nutmeg

¼ tsp ground ginger

2 cups packed brown sugar

½ cup butter, at room temperature

4 eggs, beaten

1 cup sour cream

Icing

1 cup icing sugar, sifted after measuring

2–3 Tbsp milk (2% or homogenized)

½ tsp pure vanilla extract

½ cup walnut pieces

Preheat the oven to 350°F. Butter a 5 × 9-inch loaf pan and sprinkle it with flour.

In a medium bowl, add the flour, baking soda, cinnamon, cloves, allspice, nutmeg, and ginger, and stir to combine.

To a separate larger bowl, cream together the brown sugar and butter. Add the eggs and sour cream and mix well to combine. Add the dry ingredients and stir together, taking care to not overmix.

Bake for 45 minutes or until the centre of the loaf springs back to the touch. Check for doneness by inserting a toothpick into the centre. If it comes out clean, remove the loaf from the oven and set the pan on a cooling rack for 20 minutes. When cool to the touch, ease the loaf out of the pan and set directly onto the rack for another 10 minutes.

Icing

To a small bowl, add the sifted icing sugar, 2 Tbsp of the milk, and the vanilla. Stir well until everything is combined. If you would like the icing to be thinner, add the remaining milk and stir again to combine. Drizzle over the cake and scatter the cake with walnut pieces.

When completely cool, store in a lidded container. This cake will keep in the fridge for up to 1 week.

TEA-INFUSED CRÈME ANGLAISE
WITH ROASTED FRUIT

SERVES 4

DC: This, my friends, is one of my very favourite dessert recipes for the cooler months of the year. Not only are the flavours of a black tea–infused crème anglaise (think London Fog vibes) unexpected, but also the layering of the sauce with the fruit and the sweet, buttery, and crispy "crouton" add a beautiful texture to each spoonful. I like serving this in a stemless wine glass to give it a verrine-style presentation that makes the dessert both sound and look more fancy than the effort it took to make. Gotta love an easy yet impressive end to a dinner party!

Crème Anglaise

¾ cup half and half cream

1 Tbsp good-quality black tea blend (I use Saskatoon's Be Magic Loose Leaf Teas High Tea blend)

¼ tsp pure vanilla extract

4 large egg yolks

½ cup granulated sugar

Croutons and Fruit

1 Tbsp butter, at room temperature

2 slices traditional white bread, crusts removed

1 Tbsp granulated sugar

1 Spartan apple, cored and halved

1 Bartlett pear, cored and halved

¼ cup fresh or frozen Saskatoon berries, thawed if using frozen (blueberries work here too)

Crème Anglaise

Place the cream, tea, and vanilla in a medium heat-safe bowl, and place over a pot that is one-quarter full of simmering water (this is a double boiler). Make sure the bowl itself does not touch the water; you want the steam to do the indirect heating for you! Once the cream starts to steam, stir it once gently and let the tea steep for 2–3 minutes to allow the flavour to infuse. The cream will darken in colour slightly as the tea steeps. Strain through a fine-mesh sieve into a medium bowl. Discard the tea leaves.

In a separate bowl, whisk together the egg yolks and sugar. Whisking quickly, add several spoonfuls of the hot cream mixture to the yolks to temper them, then pour the yolks directly into the hot cream and continue whisking until the mixture is thick enough to coat the back of a spoon, 4–5 minutes.

Keep warm on the stove in a pot over the lowest heat setting possible until you are ready to assemble the dessert.

Croutons and Fruit

Preheat the oven to 400°F. Line a baking sheet with parchment paper.

Spread the butter on one side of the bread slices and sprinkle the sugar evenly overtop. Cut into 1-inch cubes.

Place the prepared bread on one side of the prepared baking sheet and the apple and pear on the other. Roast in the oven until the fruit is tender and the bread is crisp, with golden brown bottoms, 15–18 minutes.

Allow the croutons and fruit to cool slightly. Cut each piece of fruit into four equal pieces.

To assemble, add the warm crème anglaise to four wine glasses, then evenly distribute the croutons and fruit among the glasses. Finish with a small spoonful of Saskatoon berries and serve immediately.

ALBERTA SOUR

SERVES 1

TC: From a cocktail perspective, the cooler days of fall are often reflected in what we put in our glass. Gin and vodka have had their day in the sun; now it's time for brown spirits like dark rum and whisky to shine. With that in mind, we've combined a southern Alberta whisky and locally made chai-flavoured bitters to create a delicious Prairie version of the Boston Sour. Sea buckthorn juice keeps it zippy while the simple syrup and frothy egg white help round out this silky-smooth classic cocktail.

2 oz Rupert's Whisky

¾ oz Sea Buckthorn Juice (page 260)

¾ oz Basic Simple Syrup (page 273)

¾ oz egg white (see note)

3 drops of Calder Chai Token Bitters

Lemon peel, ½ inch wide and 2 inches long, pith removed

Add the whisky, sea buckthorn juice, simple syrup, and egg white to a cocktail shaker and dry shake (no ice) for 30 seconds. Add a handful of ice and shake again for another 30 seconds. Strain into a chilled coupe, or into a rocks glass filled with fresh ice. Add a few drops of the bitters to the top and garnish with the lemon peel.

NOTE: *The white of one egg is approximately ¾ oz.*

DAN'S DIRTY GIBSON

SERVES 1

DC: This drink has seen me through the good, the bad, and the ugly . . . and the fun. Jokes aside, drinking a stiff martini before dinner makes me think of what my grandmother would have done while preparing to entertain friends back in the 1960s or 1970s. Most people know what a dirty martini is, but not everyone has heard of the Gibson—a slight spin on the aforementioned, using sour pickled onions instead of olives. I am a pickle fanatic, so the two briny worlds of olives and pickled onions combine into a match made in heaven.

2 oz good-quality locally made vodka or London dry–style gin (I like Anohka)

1 bar spoon dry vermouth

2 sour pickled pearl onions

1 pimento-stuffed green olive

1 bar spoon pickled pearl onion brine (for extra dirty, optional)

1–2 sour pickled pearl onions, for garnish

1–2 pimento-stuffed green olives, for garnish

Fill a martini glass with ice and water and allow to chill while preparing the drink.

Place the vodka, vermouth, onions, olive, and brine in a martini shaker, fill with ice, cover, and shake vigorously for 20 seconds.

Discard the ice water from the martini glass and strain the cocktail from the shaker into the glass. Garnish with the desired number of onions and olives (the dirtier the better?).

WINTER

MINUS 30 DOESN'T SCARE US.

The Prairies may evoke images of flat lands where howling winds create snowdrifts as high as cars, but "it's a dry cold," as they say. We're ready—we've preserved and canned and made syrups and jellies. Our freezers are stocked with fruit and vegetables picked at the height of the season. Big fat birds and cuts of beef and pork purchased from farmers are nestled right alongside them, wrapped and at the ready to be braised and roasted and turned into nutritious broth. And still, the earth produces.

Brussels sprouts are sweeter after the first frost, and root vegetables, while still considered the fuddy-duddies of the dirt, can yield the most wonderful results when properly cooked. These are the vegetables that sustained Eastern European immigrants accustomed to the short summers and harsh winters of the Old Country. Those vegetables, and their cousins like cabbage and kohlrabi, persisted then, as they do now, across the Canadian Prairies. Come December, they are what take up real estate in our cellars along with varieties of winter squash ready to prove their versatility in everything from soups to desserts.

Winter is coming. We got this.

HEMP HUMMUS

MAKES 2 CUPS

TC: A hemp heart is the tender inside of a hemp seed. While you can eat the entire seed, including the hard, high-fibre shell, the heart is softer and therefore easier to incorporate into dishes. Hemp hearts are packed with protein, iron, and omega-3 fatty acids, which makes them a natural nutritional supplement.

You can add hemp hearts to almost anything—baked goods, soup, smoothies, yogurt, salad, and dips. The hearts have a nutty flavour, and when ground into a paste, add depth and a creamy texture to a dip, like hummus. In this recipe, lemon juice is key, as no other acidity comes close in zippiness or flavour. As far as the oil component goes, you won't miss the olive oil, because the cold-pressed canola oil is full of Prairie terroir. The deep golden colour that makes this oil so beautiful makes it ideal for a dish like this that just wants a little ooh-la-la without going overboard.

While hemp is grown nationwide, the Prairie provinces are responsible for almost 90% of Canada's production. You'll find hemp products in most grocery stores, natural food stores, and even in the cookware section of select home decor stores.

4 Tbsp hulled hemp hearts

2 Tbsp lemon juice

1 can (19 oz) chickpeas, drained and rinsed

3 Tbsp water, plus more as needed

2 cloves garlic (small), peeled and halved

3 Tbsp regular canola oil

2 Tbsp + 1 tsp cold-pressed canola

1 tsp kosher salt

1 pinch mild Hungarian paprika

1 tsp chopped fresh flat-leaf parsley

Place the hemp hearts in a mortar and use a pestle to grind them into a loose paste.

To a small food processor, add the hemp paste, lemon juice, chickpeas, water, garlic, regular canola oil, 2 Tbsp of the cold-pressed canola oil, and the salt. Blend for 1 minute or until smooth. If you want thinner hummus, add up to 1 Tbsp more of water.

Serve the hummus in a bowl or shallow dish and finish with the remaining 1 tsp cold-pressed canola drizzled overtop along with a sprinkling of paprika and the parsley.

ROASTED GOLDEN BEETS WITH FRESH CHEESE AND TOASTED HAZELNUTS

SERVES 4

TC: Golden beets were first offered for commercial sale in the 1940s but remained relatively unknown until the 1990s, when they started appearing on restaurant menus. Up until then, it was the earthy-flavoured red beet that people had been pickling and making into soup. Golden and Chioggia beets have a sweeter, more subtle flavour than the red variety and are wonderful when roasted and sprinkled with sea salt.

Beets and soft cheese are a delicious combination, and finishing with a sprinkling of chopped nuts adds a lovely textural element to this dish. We use the fromage blanc made by Ian Truer at Lakeside Dairy, north of Edmonton, but a freshly made ricotta like our MRKT Fresh Ricotta (page 258) would also work well.

½ cup unsalted hazelnuts

2 tsp + 1 Tbsp canola oil, divided

2 lb small golden beets (about 8-10), peeled and cut into ½-inch slices

1 Tbsp fresh rosemary

1 Tbsp finely chopped fresh sage

½ tsp sea salt

½ tsp freshly ground black pepper

¼ cup dried cranberries

1½ Tbsp Apple Cider Vinaigrette (page 269)

¾ cup fromage blanc

1 Tbsp chopped fresh flat-leaf parsley

Preheat the oven to 425°F. Line a baking sheet with parchment paper.

Spread the hazelnuts on a cutting board and coarsely chop into small pieces.

Add 2 tsp of oil to a non-stick frying pan and heat over medium heat. Add the nuts and occasionally stir until they are lightly browned. Keep an eye on them so they don't burn. This should take only a few minutes. Set aside to cool.

To a large bowl, add the beet slices and coat with the remaining 1 Tbsp oil. Add the rosemary, sage, salt, and pepper and toss to coat.

Arrange the beets in a single layer on the prepared baking sheet. Roast for 20 minutes, turning the beets at the 10-minute mark to allow for even browning. After roasting, let the beets cool for a few minutes.

To serve, place the beets in a bowl, add the cranberries, and toss with the vinaigrette. Arrange in a serving dish, sprinkle the hazelnuts over top, add dollops of the cheese, and garnish with the parsley.

SHAVED BRUSSELS AND BREAD SALAD

SERVES 4

DC: Talented chef Garrett Martin expands our horizons with this rewarding recipe that gets a hefty flavour boost thanks to some flavourful cheese and a punch of coarsely ground black pepper.

"This dish pairs nicely with roasted chicken or pork, but it stands up well by itself as well. Be generous with the black pepper, as it helps add a necessary spice to the dish. The crunchy exterior and the soft interior for the croutons is a necessary texture to bring this dish to life." —Garrett Martin, executive chef at Major Tom

Honey Mustard Vinaigrette

2 Tbsp apple cider vinegar

2 tsp wildflower honey (or other good-quality local honey)

1 Tbsp whole-grain Dijon mustard

1 Tbsp water

¼ cup canola oil

¼ tsp salt

Croutons

2 Tbsp butter

2 Tbsp canola oil

2 thick slices of good-quality sourdough bread, torn into ½-inch pieces

Kosher salt

Assembly

4 cups of very thinly sliced raw Brussels sprouts (about 16–20 trimmed sprouts)

1 cup coarsely grated Kootenay Alpine Cheese Co. Nostrala (or a good-quality Gouda), divided

1 Tbsp coarsely ground black pepper

Honey Mustard Vinaigrette

Add the vinegar, honey, mustard, water, oil, and salt to a container with a tight-fitting lid and shake the container vigorously until the mixture is emulsified.

Croutons

Preheat the oven to 375°F.

In a large, oven-safe pan, melt the butter and oil until the butter begins to bubble. Add the bread and toss to coat it, then season generously with salt. Transfer the pan to the oven and toast the croutons until they're crispy on the outside but still a little tender in the middle, 7–10 minutes. Set aside.

Assembly

In a large mixing bowl, combine the Brussels sprouts, vinaigrette, croutons, ¾ cup of the cheese, and the black pepper. (Go even heavier on the pepper if you like; it's a delicious complement to the cheese!) Taste and adjust the seasoning with more salt and pepper if necessary.

Let the salad sit for a minute or two before serving to soften the croutons a bit. Transfer to a platter or individual bowls and finish with remaining ¼ cup cheese and some black pepper.

CHARRED RED AND GREEN CABBAGE WITH HONEY BÉARNAISE

SERVES 4

DC: A plate of beautifully charred cabbage may be the exemplar of contemporary Prairie cooking. Using intense heat adds amazing depth of flavour and umami to a common—and still widely inexpensive—winter vegetable, transforming cabbage into a true showstopper, especially for people who look at it as a mundane ingredient. Old-school French chefs may balk at this version of béarnaise that incorporates unique locally made vinegar and honey, but I think it's pretty spectacular.

Honey Béarnaise

⅓ cup Alchemist Vinegar Honey Chive Vinegar (or apple cider vinegar)

1 tsp unpasteurized honey

3 Tbsp diced shallot

2 Tbsp finely chopped tarragon, divided

3 large egg yolks

1 cup hot melted butter

Salt

Charred Cabbage

¼ small red cabbage, cut into ½-inch-thick pieces

¼ small green cabbage, cut into ½-inch-thick pieces

¼ cup canola oil

Salt

Honey Béarnaise

Place the vinegar, honey, shallot, and 1 Tbsp of the tarragon in a small pot over medium heat. Stir to combine and cook until the liquid has almost fully reduced and the shallots are very tender, about 5 minutes. Remove from the heat and allow to cool in the pot to near room temperature before adding the egg yolks. Stir well with a spoon to combine.

Using an immersion blender, purée the mixture directly in the pot while slowly adding the melted butter (the butter should be hot to the touch, but not scalding). Once all the butter has been added, you should be left with a smooth, viscous sauce. Season to taste with salt. Stir in the remaining 1 Tbsp tarragon, cover, and keep on the stove over the lowest heat setting until ready to serve.

Charred Cabbage

Preheat the oven to 425°F.

Lay the cabbage pieces in one layer on a baking sheet. Using a pastry brush, top each piece with oil and season liberally with salt.

Roast until the cabbage is tender and browned on top with crispy edges, about 20 minutes. Turn the temperature to broil and cook for 3–4 minutes more to allow the caramelization to intensify. Pay attention here, as you want the tops of the cabbage to darken notably, but not burn.

Assembly

Spoon a generous layer of warm honey béarnaise onto the base of a serving dish and top with pieces of green and red cabbage. Serve any extra béarnaise on the side for extra indulgence!

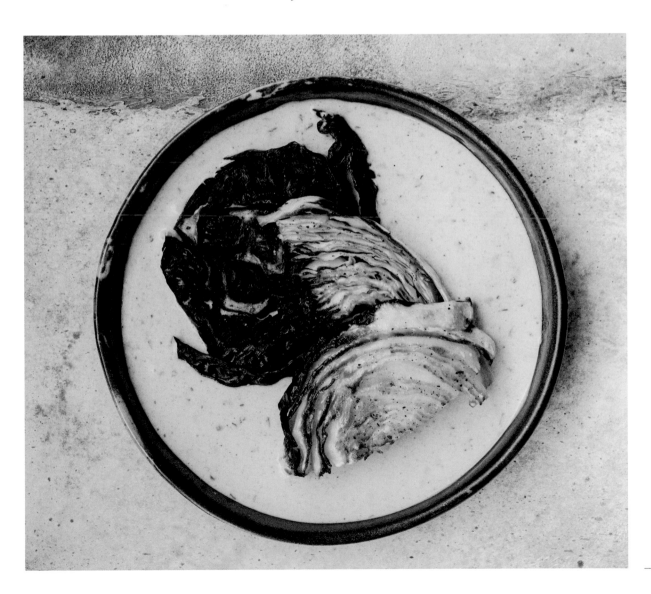

ROAST CHICKEN, CABBAGE, AND LENTIL SALAD

SERVES 4–5

DC: Whenever I'm travelling abroad, I'm always curious to see what Canadian-grown items I can find at a local grocery store. This dish was born of this curiosity when I was visiting friends in Prague and was tasked with making dinner one night. At the nearby grocer, I found Saskatchewan-grown green lentils and Canadian maple syrup and decided to try my hand at making a rich-tasting salad that evening. It turned out to be a hit, and it's been one of my go-to winter recipes for the past few years.

4 Tbsp canola oil, divided

3 Tbsp maple syrup, divided

½ tsp coarsely ground black pepper

4 skin-on, bone-in chicken thighs

½ cup water

¼ small green cabbage, cut into ¼-inch-thick slices

Salt

3 cups cooked whole green lentils

3 Tbsp finely chopped fresh chives

2 Tbsp apple cider vinegar

1 Tbsp grainy Dijon mustard

1 pinch chili flakes

Preheat the oven to 400°F.

In a small bowl, whisk together 2 Tbsp of the oil, 2 Tbsp of the maple syrup, and the pepper.

Place the chicken thighs in a small baking dish. Drizzle the syrup mixture over the meat and roast for 20 minutes. Add the water to the bottom of the baking dish, and use a baster to incorporate the water with the drippings and syrup mixture. Baste the thighs and continue to roast the chicken, until cooked through and the skin is crispy, about 15 minutes more.

Transfer the roasted chicken to paper towel to cool and absorb any excess grease. Strain the pan drippings into a small bowl and set aside. Once the chicken has cooled, remove the meat from the bones and chop coarsely.

Lightly toss the cabbage with the remaining 2 Tbsp oil, season with salt, and use the same baking dish to roast in the oven until slightly charred and tender, about 30 minutes. Let cool to just above room temperature. Chop coarsely and combine in a large bowl with the chicken, lentils, and chives.

Pour the reserved pan-drippings into a pot along with the remaining 1 Tbsp maple syrup and the vinegar, mustard, and chili flakes and cook on medium heat for 5 minutes or until the mixture has reduced by one-third.

Pour the pan-dripping vinaigrette over the salad and toss until well coated. The salad can be served slightly warm or cold. If you're serving this dish cold, do not add the chicken until just before dining so the skin does not get too soggy.

DILL PICKLE AND LEEK SOUP

SERVES 4–5

DC: If there is someone out there in the world who loves pickles as much as I do, I would like to meet them. As you've probably noticed throughout this book, I take every opportunity to incorporate all types of pickled vegetables and their respective brines into my home cooking. You'll be hard-pressed to find a savoury dish that a little bit of brine doesn't make more delicious, and my Dill Pickle and Leek Soup is a great example of that. When you see the words "good quality" below, that really just means you should use *your* favourite type of pickles . . . just not bread and butter, okay? They have no place here or in your fridge! Like most soups in this world, this one tastes even more delicious a day or two after you make it. While dill pickles are obviously a year-round affair, cellared leeks usually peter out by mid-winter, so best make the most of the locally grown tender buttery alliums.

1 Tbsp canola oil

2 medium leeks, dark green ends and root trimmed, halved, and thinly sliced (about 3 cups)

1½ cups grated good-quality dill pickles

2 medium russet potatoes, peeled and diced (about 3 cups)

1 cup brine from good-quality dill pickles

1 cup + 2 Tbsp water, divided

6 cups vegetable broth

1 tsp garlic powder

½ tsp dried dill

½ tsp chili flakes

2 Tbsp all-purpose flour

2 cups half and half cream

Salt and pepper

Heat the oil in a medium pot over medium-high heat. Add the leeks and cook until softened, 5–6 minutes. Add the pickles, potatoes, brine, 1 cup of the water, broth, garlic powder, dried dill, and chili flakes. Once the soup comes to a simmer, reduce the heat to medium and simmer for 20 minutes, stirring occasionally.

In a small bowl, stir together the flour and remaining 2 Tbsp water to form a slurry and add to the pot. Stir and the soup should thicken noticeably. Add the cream, then let the soup return to a simmer and cook for another 10 minutes.

Season to taste with salt and pepper and serve. This soup can keep in the fridge for up to 1 week and, if stored in a freezer-safe container, in the freezer for up to 3 months.

NOTE: *To keep this soup vegan, add an extra cup of diced potatoes and 2 additional cups of vegetable broth instead of the cream. Purée to achieve a similar creamy consistency as in the recipe above.*

BISON CABBAGE ROLL SOUP

SERVES 6

DC: Cabbage rolls are one of the most beloved comfort foods you'll find in the Prairies. Many folks here have Ukrainian family roots, so a made-with-love-by-somebody's-baba batch of cabbage rolls is never more than a stone's throw away. This soup is an ode to the dish, but further embraces Prairie ingredients by using ground bison instead of beef, as well as sage and a little chili vodka from a popular Saskatoon distillery for a little kick. *Budmo!*

1 Tbsp canola oil

½ cup diced pancetta

1 yellow onion, diced

4 cloves garlic, minced

¼ cup chili vodka (I like Lucky Bastard Horilka)

2 lb ground bison

3 Tbsp tomato paste

1 can (14 oz) diced tomatoes

4 cups vegetable broth

4 cups beef broth

1 cup water

3 cups sauerkraut

¾ cup uncooked white long-grain rice

1 tsp finely fresh chopped sage

Salt

Chopped fresh flat-leaf parsley, for garnish

Hand-Torn Garlic Bread (page 263, optional)

Heat the oil in a large pot on medium-high heat. Add the pancetta and cook until the fat starts to release, about 1 minute. Add the onion and garlic and cook for 10 minutes, stirring occasionally. Once small brown bits start to form on the bottom of the pot, add splashes of the vodka to help deglaze. If you haven't used all the vodka in this process, pour in the remainder before moving on to the next step.

Add the bison and tomato paste to the pot and let the meat brown, stirring occasionally, 4–5 minutes. Add the diced tomatoes, vegetable broth, beef broth, water, sauerkraut, rice, and sage. Stir well and let the soup come to a simmer. Once bubbling, reduce to the heat to low, cover, and cook for 40 minutes.

Remove the lid and season to taste with salt. Continue to cook for 10 minutes, uncovered, to allow the soup to reduce slightly and the flavours to further mingle. Ladle out, top with parsley, and serve with warm garlic bread.

THE ULTIMATE TURKEY DINNER LEFTOVERS SOUP

SERVES 4–6

DC: First of all, do not go making big batches of mashed potatoes, carrots, and roast turkey just to make this soup. This recipe is meant for you to look at your leftovers as a mise en place for something "new." This baked soup is *always* a hit in my household. It's an unexpected way to use leftovers, but once you consider that broth plus cream plus mashed potatoes add up to what is essentially cream of potato soup, adding a few extra vegetables and turkey meat isn't so odd at all.

Soup Topping

2½ cups leftover stuffing

½ cup finely grated parmesan cheese

½ cup grated mozzarella

¼ cup heavy (35%) cream

Soup

2 Tbsp canola oil

2 yellow onions, diced

6 cups turkey broth (or chicken broth)

2 cups leftover mashed potatoes

½ cup leftover gravy

1 Tbsp apple cider vinegar

1 tsp dried rosemary

1 cup chopped leftover carrots (or other winter vegetable like parsnips, acorn squash, or butternut squash)

1 cup finely chopped leftover cooked turkey meat

¼ cup heavy (35%) cream

Salt

Soup Topping

Place the stuffing, parmesan, mozzarella, and cream in a medium bowl and mix gently to combine.

Soup

Heat the oil in a large pot over medium-high heat. Add the onions and cook for 5 minutes, stirring occasionally. Add the broth, potatoes, gravy, vinegar, and rosemary. Once the mixture comes to a simmer, reduce to the heat to low and use an immersion blender to purée until smooth.

Add the carrots, turkey, and cream and continue to cook until near-simmering. Season to taste with salt.

Preheat the oven to 375°F.

Fill six heat-safe bowls with soup, and divide the soup topping evenly among the bowls. Bake for 10 minutes, then broil on high for 2–3 minutes, until the topping has turned golden brown and crispy.

Allow the soup to cool for several minutes before serving. If there are any soup leftovers, well, you missed the whole point of this recipe in the first place!

ACORN SQUASH AND CHEDDAR FRITTATA

SERVES 4–5

DC: I love a weekend brunch moment, and there is no better blank canvas to get creative with in the a.m. than a frittata. With a foundation of eggs and milk (or cream), a basic frittata welcomes all kinds of flavours into the fold. This recipe uses greenhouse-grown cherry tomatoes—because dead of winter—and acorn squash . . . with the peel on. If you've never done this before, trust us that it is absolutely edible and adds some nice texture. People don't often think of comfort food when it comes to breakfast or brunch, but with this warming meal I say: Why the heck not?

1 Tbsp unsalted butter

⅛ small acorn squash, skin on and thinly sliced

8 eggs

⅓ cup whole milk or half and half cream

¼ cup coarsely chopped fresh basil

1 cup grated mild cheddar (I like Lakeside Dairy)

1 tsp hot sauce (I like Knockout Heat Co. Red Habanero Hot Sauce) (optional)

½ tsp sea salt

6 cherry tomatoes, thinly sliced

4–6 fresh sage leaves

Preheat the oven to 400°F.

Heat the butter in a large pan over medium-high heat. Once melted and beginning to sizzle, add the squash and cook for 3–4 minutes, stirring occasionally, until slightly softened. Remove from the heat and let cool.

Place the eggs, milk, basil, cheese, hot sauce, and salt in a large mixing bowl, and whisk to combine. Pour the mixture into a 9 × 9-inch baking dish or an oven-safe 10-to-12-inch skillet. Disperse the squash, tomatoes, and sage leaves evenly across the surface of the egg mixture.

Bake for 40 minutes or until the frittata is lightly browned on top and completely cooked through in the centre. To check this, press lightly on the centre of the frittata with a spoon. It should be fairly firm with a bit of bounce when pressed. Let cool slightly before serving.

NOTE: *The frittata can be prepped 1 day ahead, covered, and kept in the fridge. When ready to bake, allow the mixture to come to room temperature before baking.*

RUTABAGA, HAM, AND POTATO BAKE

SERVES 4–6

DC: In my house, scalloped potatoes haven't just gotten a facelift, they wound up getting some filler too . . . and that's not a bad thing. I'm a big fan of using a little less potato and a little more rutabaga—one of the most neglected vegetables in the world. Its earthy-sweet-and-slightly-bitter flavour profile breathes new life into an otherwise predictable winter recipe. Well, that and my winter-spiced cream which, I assure you, is an absolutely game changer for most comfort-food recipes that call for cream. Why? Steeping the cream in a wide array of aromatics acts as a pronounced flavour booster. It's a trick I like to use for things like mashed potatoes, cream-based pasta sauces, and more. This dish is best served with a "main affair" like roast turkey. In other words, it is a wonderful side dish for a holiday dinner.

Winter-Spiced Cream

2 cups heavy (35%) cream

3 shallots, coarsely chopped

2 cloves garlic

6 black peppercorns

4 allspice berries

2 whole cloves

1 cinnamon stick

1 whole nutmeg seed

2 cups grated jersey milk Gouda (or regular Gouda)

2 Tbsp cornstarch

2 Tbsp water

Salt

Rutabaga, Ham, and Potato Bake

1 medium rutabaga, peeled and sliced into ¼-inch rounds

2 medium red potatoes, sliced into ¼-inch rounds

1 lb smoked boneless ham, sliced ¼ inch thick

Winter-Spiced Cream

Combine the cream, shallots, garlic, peppercorns, allspice, cloves, cinnamon, and nutmeg in a medium pot and bring to a near-simmer over medium heat. Once the mixture is steaming, but not simmering, reduce the heat to low and cover. Let the cream steep for 20–25 minutes to allow the flavours to infuse.

Uncover, strain into a medium bowl through a fine-mesh sieve, and discard all aromatics. Return the liquid to the pot, increase the heat to medium, and stir in the Gouda until melted.

Whisk together the cornstarch and water in a small bowl to form a slurry, and then pour the slurry into the cream mixture. Stir constantly while allowing the contents of the pot to thicken, approximately 1 minute. Season to taste with salt and set aside until you are ready to assemble and bake the complete dish.

continued on next page

⅓ cup melted butter

½ tsp dried basil

1 cup grated jersey milk Gouda
(or regular Gouda)

Rutabaga, Ham, and Potato Bake

Preheat the oven to 375°F.

Place the rutabaga, potatoes, ham, butter, and basil in a large mixing bowl and toss to combine. Transfer to a 9 × 9-inch baking dish and pour the winter-spiced cream over top. Top with the cheese.

Bake for 45 minutes. At this point, the contents of the dish should be tender–check by piercing with a knife. If the knife slides in easily, it is cooked through. If not, continue to bake for a few more minutes.

Turn the oven temperature to broil and cook until the top of the dish turns golden brown and bubbly, 4–5 minutes. Let cool for several minutes before serving. Leftovers can be stored in a sealed container for up to 1 week.

BEET MEZZALUNE

SERVES 4

DC: Christie Peters uses Saskatchewan ingredients to create stunning Italian-style dishes. This dish uses locally grown beets and cheese along with preserved onions and cured Saskatchewan trout to finish.

"I chose the mezzaluna shape because it reminded me of a perogy, which is synonymous with food culture here on the Prairies." —Christie Peters, co-owner of Primal and Pop Wine Bar

Beet Filling

18 oz canned (or cooked) beets, drained, patted dry, and coarsely chopped

⅓ cup melted unsalted butter

1½ cups mascarpone cheese

½ tsp salt

1 Tbsp red wine vinegar

Pasta Dough

½ cup olive oil

12 medium eggs

15 egg yolks

1 tsp salt

1.25 kg all-purpose flour, plus more for dusting

Assembly

16 thin slices of cured trout (about 8 oz)

Pickled onions, for garnish (optional)

¼ cup melted butter

2 tsp poppy seeds, for garnish

2 Tbsp finely sliced green onions, for garnish

Beet Filling

Place the beets and melted butter in a blender and purée on high until smooth. Transfer to a large mixing bowl and combine with the mascarpone. Season to taste with the salt and vinegar. Transfer the filling to a piping bag and set aside until ready to fill the mezzalune.

Pasta Dough

In a medium bowl, whisk the oil into the eggs, yolks, and salt. Place the flour in a stand mixer or on a clean surface. Mix with the hook attachment or form a well and mix by hand. Stir while slowly incorporating the egg mixture until the dough comes together–it will have a texture similar to bread dough. Vacuum seal the dough or wrap it in plastic wrap and let it rest.

Section the dough into four pieces. Flatten each portion into a rectangular shape (the ideal shape to fit through your pasta sheet roller). Cover both sides with a dusting of flour.

Set your pasta sheet roller to #1. In batches, run each portion of dough through the pasta sheet roller. With the setting on #1, fold the dough in half and run it through again. Repeat the folding in half and rolling at least four more times.

continued on next page

Once you've run the dough through the #1 setting several times, flour both sides of the dough and change the pasta sheet roller to #2. Run the pasta through the #2 setting two times. Change the setting to #3 and run it through once. Change the setting to #4 and run it through one more time. Finally, put it to the #5 setting and roll it through once. You should be able to see light through the dough if you hold it up. It is now thin enough to work.

Cut out rounds of the dough with a 3-to-4-inch round cutter, then pipe your filling into the centre, about 1 tsp. Spritz with water or use your finger to wet half of the circle's edge, then gently fold the dough in half over the filling and press closed with your fingertips, being careful not to trap any air by pressing as close to the filling as possible. Use a fork to press them shut, giving them the signature ridges.

Place the finished mezzalune on a parchment-lined floured baking sheet and cover with a clean damp dish towel until ready to cook. At this point they can also be placed in a sealed container or plastic bag and frozen for use another day. If packaged in freezer-durable packaging, they will keep for up to 3 months. Repeat until you've used all your filling or dough (you can save and re-roll the scraps of dough as well if you like).

Assembly

Fill a large pot to the halfway point with water. Add enough salt so that it tastes like the sea and bring to a boil.

Working in several batches, cook the pasta in the boiling water until al dente, 2–3 minutes when cooked from fresh. If you are cooking the mezzalune from frozen, allow to cook for an additional 45 seconds to 1 minute.

Transfer to a serving platter or portion out onto individual plates. Top with the cured trout, onions, melted butter, poppy seeds, and green onions.

PARSNIP POTATO PURÉE WITH VEGETABLE GRAVY

SERVES 4

TC: I'm not sure why the parsnip doesn't get the respect it deserves. This cousin of the carrot keeps its shape when cooked, which makes it perfect for bulking up soups and stews, and because parsnips have a sweet, nutty flavour, they're ideal for roasting: you don't have to do much other than drizzle with canola oil, roast, and finish with flaky sea salt. That unique flavour, when added to mashed potatoes, takes the potatoes from flat to fabulous, which is what happens in this recipe. Top puréed parsnips with a savoury sauce like vegetable gravy, and you've got the perfect side for baked ham or holiday turkey.

Parsnip Potato Purée

1 lb parsnips, peeled and cut into 1-inch pieces

2 large russet potatoes, peeled and cubed

1 cup buttermilk

3 sprigs fresh thyme

4 Tbsp butter

½ tsp salt

½ tsp white pepper

Vegetable Gravy

¼ cup butter

1 small yellow onion, diced

½ cup all-purpose flour

4 cups Roasted Vegetable Broth (page 264)

1 Tbsp nutritional yeast

½ tsp white pepper

2 tsp Worcestershire sauce

1 Tbsp soy sauce

½ Tbsp tomato paste

Parsnip Potato Purée

Add the parsnips and potatoes to a large pot of boiling water and cook for 20 minutes or until tender.

In a separate saucepan, heat the buttermilk to just warm–do not let it boil. Add the thyme and let it steep in the hot liquid for 10 minutes.

Drain the parsnips and potatoes and turn the heat off. Add the parsnips and potatoes back to the pot, place on the stove, and let the residual heat dry up the remaining moisture. Transfer the parsnips and potatoes to a bowl.

Set a ricer over the used pot on the element and rice the parsnips and potatoes 2 cups at a time. With the heat still turned off, add the butter, salt, and pepper to the riced parsnip mixture. Remove the thyme from the buttermilk, then add half of the milk to the mixture, stirring constantly with a spatula. Add the remaining milk and stir until creamy. Turn the heat to low, cover, and stir once or twice while making the gravy.

Vegetable Gravy

Melt the butter in a medium saucepan over medium heat. When it foams, add the onion and sauté for a few minutes, until translucent. Add the flour and whisk to combine. Keep stirring until the roux starts to lightly brown. You don't want it to brown too much, so watch the heat.

Slowly add the broth and keep stirring. Once everything is combined, incorporate the nutritional yeast, pepper, Worcestershire sauce, soy sauce, and tomato paste and whisk for 1 minute or until the sauce is thick enough to coat the back of a spoon.

If the sauce is too thick, stir in 1 Tbsp of hot water. Taste and season with more salt, if needed.

Keep the sauce in the pot, covered and over low heat. When ready to serve, transfer to a gravy boat, place alongside the bowl of puréed parsnips and potatoes, and let guests help themselves.

NOTE: *If the parsnips are large, quarter them lengthwise and cut out the woody core, otherwise they will be difficult to mash to a nice consistency. If they're small, simply peel and cut them into evenly sized rounds.*

ELK MEATBALLS

SERVES 4

TC: On sausage-making day, my parents would set aside some of the pork and beef mixture to form into patties and fry up on the woodstove for lunch. The meat came from animals we raised, and to this day, I can instantly recall how wonderful those patties tasted, seasoned only with fresh garlic, salt, and pepper. When you work with quality meat, you don't need to mess around with a lot of extra seasonings. Let the meat speak for itself.

The Butchery by Rge Rd, in Edmonton, carries locally raised meat, including elk that is farmed in central Alberta by Kyle Stephenson. It's a wonderful meat to work with, but it is lean, so it needs a bit of help from a fattier meat, like pork. I love to serve these meatballs with the Parsnip Potato Purée with Vegetable Gravy (page 164), or use them to make a meatball sub.

1 day-old bread roll or bun

1 Tbsp + ½ cup canola oil, divided

1 medium onion, diced

2 cloves garlic, minced

10 oz ground pork

10 oz ground elk (see note)

1 egg

3 Tbsp finely chopped fresh flat-leaf parsley

1½ tsp kosher salt

1 tsp freshly ground black pepper

Soak the bread in about ½ cup of water for 15 minutes. Drain the water and squeeze out the excess, and crumble the bread into a large bowl.

While the bread is soaking, add 1 Tbsp of canola oil to a frying pan, heat over medium heat, and sauté the onion for about 10 minutes, making sure to stir often. Turn the heat to medium-low, add the garlic, and cook for 5 minutes more, until the garlic is softened.

To the soaked breadcrumbs, add the pork, elk, egg, parsley, salt, and pepper. When the onion is cool enough to handle, add it and mix well to combine.

Keeping your hands wet, roll the meat mixture into ping-pong-sized balls. The meatballs can be either fried or baked.

To Fry

Add ¼ cup of oil to a deep non-stick frying pan and heat over medium heat. Add the meatballs, five or six at a time, and cook for about 15 minutes, turning the meatballs as they cook. Use the remaining ¼ cup oil for frying, if needed.

continued on next page

Preheat the oven to 375°F and line a baking sheet with parchment paper or a silicone baking mat. Place the meatballs on the prepared baking sheet and bake for 10 minutes, then, using tongs, turn the meatballs over and cook for another 10 minutes.

Transfer the meatballs to a platter and serve with mashed potatoes or our Parsnip Potato Purée with Vegetable Gravy. They're also great added to an Italian-style tomato sauce and served over pasta.

Leftover meatballs can be stored in a sealed container in the fridge for up 2 days, or in the freezer for up to 1 month. Raw meatballs freeze well too. Just place the raw meatballs on a parchment-lined baking sheet and freeze until solid. Transfer the frozen meatballs to a container or zip-lock bag and take out as needed. Cook them from frozen by placing them on a parchment-lined baking sheet in a 375°F preheated oven for 25–30 minutes, or until they reach an internal temperature of 160°F. Turning them a few times while they cook will ensure they are evenly browned.

NOTE: *If you have trouble sourcing elk, bison will work just as well. If neither is available, ground beef will work too, but because of the ground pork in this recipe, I recommend using lean ground beef, not regular.*

COWBOY COUNTRY BEEF ROAST
WITH SMOKED GARLIC GRAVY

SERVES 6-8

TC: Our Prairies are filled with farmers and ranchers who know that if you don't take care of the soil first, nothing will grow, and that means not only the crops and plants, but the livestock too. There is a reason why Canadian beef has a stellar reputation around the globe—the proof is in the flavour.

Speaking of flavour, we're using our Cowboy Country Spice Rub (page 271) and some smoked garlic purée from Fifth Gen Gardens to take classic beef roast with gravy to the next level. You'll want to go online and order some of that garlic purée. It is wickedly delicious. If you don't use this particular ingredient, you can find regular puréed garlic at your local grocery store, although the end result will be missing that deeper smoky aspect. Wondering about sides? Pickled beets are an automatic pairing for me (it's what Mom always served), so if you've made Spicy Pickled Beets (page 84), you're all set. If not, the Roasted Golden Beets with Fresh Cheese and Toasted Hazelnuts (page 142) will deliver that robust earthiness while acting as a heartier culinary complement.

Beef Roast

3 lb sirloin beef roast, tied

2 Tbsp Cowboy Country Spice Rub (page 271)

½ cup Fifth Gen Gardens smoked garlic purée

Gravy

4 cups vegetable or beef broth, at room temperature

3 Tbsp butter

½ cup all-purpose flour, plus more as needed

1 tsp kosher salt

Beef Roast

Preheat the oven to 450°F and remove the roast from the fridge, allowing it to come to room temperature for 30 minutes.

Place the roast in a shallow dish, coat with the spice rub, and rub it in. Dollop the garlic onto the roast and use the back of a spoon to spread evenly over the entire surface.

Place the roast on a rack inside a roasting pan and roast for 20 minutes uncovered. Turn the heat down to 325°F and roast until the internal temperature reaches 145°F for medium-rare. (For medium-rare, a 3 lb roast will take 1¾–2 hours to cook.) Remove the roast from the pan, set it in a shallow dish, and tent with tinfoil while you prepare the gravy—save the pan drippings!

continued on next page

Gravy

With the heat off, add the broth to the pan drippings and stir with a wooden spoon to loosen the brown bits and drippings. Transfer the liquid to a 6-cup pot or pitcher and set aside.

To make the roux, melt the butter in a medium saucepan over medium heat. Add the flour and whisk to combine, until the mixture is crumbly but still moist. If the roux looks too loose, add more flour, 1 tsp at a time. Keep whisking! You want the roux to brown, but not burn.

The roux should be a golden brown colour after about 5 minutes. When that happens, slowly add the broth and continue to whisk until the gravy is smooth. This should only take a couple of minutes. If the gravy is too thick, add a bit of water. Add the salt, taste, and add a pinch more, if needed. Pour the gravy into a small pitcher or gravy boat and place it on the table.

Transfer the roast to a cutting board. Stir the juice that's left behind in the dish into the gravy. Use a carving knife to cut slices ¼ inch thick, and then place the slices back in the dish and serve.

NOTE: *It's vital that the beef roasts on a rack in the pan, and while the resulting drippings won't be overly abundant, what's there will be worth its weight in gold.*

KUPPERSHNUCK

SERVES 6

TC: In the late 1800s, my ancestors, along with thousands of other Eastern European immigrants, came to Canada and settled across the Prairies. The land and the food grown were like what they left behind, which made it easy to recreate dishes from the Homeland. People from Poland and Ukraine made kapusniak, a sauerkraut soup containing carrots and potatoes. The German women in my family made a similar dish but with rice, and they cooked it longer which made it more of a casserole than a soup. Because recipes were never written down, we're not sure of the spelling. We've just always spelled it like it sounds: KUP-per-shnuck. The dish is hearty enough to be a meal on its own, but it also makes a great side to roast turkey or baked ham.

1 lb bacon, chopped

1 medium onion, chopped

2 cloves garlic, minced

1 cup white long-grain rice

2 cups sauerkraut (19 oz jar)

2½ cups water

¼ tsp freshly ground black pepper

Salt

NOTE: *You can cook kuppershnuck two ways: in the oven or on the stovetop. I've described the oven method, but if you prefer the stovetop method, simply turn the heat to low after you've added the final ingredients, cover the pot, and simmer for 40 minutes.*

Preheat the oven to 350°F (see note).

To a medium (5-quart) Dutch oven over medium heat, add the bacon and cook for about 10 minutes, until the fat is rendered but the meat is still soft. Do not drain off the fat. Turn the heat to medium-low, add the onion, and cook for a few minutes, until translucent. Add the garlic and let everything sweat for a few minutes before adding the rice. Stir to ensure all the grains get a good coating of bacon fat.

Add the sauerkraut, water, pepper, and salt to taste. (If you feel your bacon is salty enough, you might want to pass on additional salt here.) Cover the pot, set in the oven, and bake for 45 minutes. If there is noticeable liquid remaining at the end of the cook time, cook for another 10 minutes. The dish should look moist—not dry to the point of making the rice grains split. Fluff before serving.

Leftover kuppershnuck can be kept in a sealed container in the fridge for up to 1 week.

NOTE: *Use some leftover meatloaf in a grilled cheese sandwich for lunch the following day and thank me later!*

MUSTARD AND BROWN SUGAR–GLAZED BEEF MEATLOAF

SERVES 4–5

DC: There is plenty of nostalgia to be found in meatloaf. It was one of the first dishes I remember making on my own as a kid, and it is a dish that has provided much comfort during many a chilly Prairie winter. I have a few meatloaf recipes in my arsenal, but this one that features Canadian beef, puréed dried red lentils, and a deliciously easy-to-make mustard and brown sugar glaze feels especially fitting for this cookbook. Enjoy this meatloaf with the Parsnip Potato Purée (page 64) for an extra-comforting meal.

Glaze

¼ cup yellow mustard

¼ cup lightly packed brown sugar

2 Tbsp butter

Meatloaf

2 Tbsp canola oil

2 yellow onions, halved and thinly sliced

2 cloves garlic, coarsely chopped

2 Tbsp tomato paste

1 Tbsp honey

2 Tbsp good-quality barbecue sauce (I like Bow Valley BBQ's Bigfoot Bold BBQ Sauce)

¾ cup + 1 Tbsp dried red lentils, puréed to a coarse texture comparable to cornmeal

2 lb lean ground beef chuck

2 eggs

1 Tbsp grainy Dijon mustard

1 tsp salt

Glaze

Combine the mustard, sugar, and butter in a small pot. Cook over medium heat until the sugar has dissolved, the butter has melted, and the glaze has a smooth consistency, 3–4 minutes. Remove from the heat and let cool.

Meatloaf

Preheat the oven to 400°F. Line a 5 × 9-inch loaf pan with parchment paper.

Heat the oil in a medium non-stick pan over medium-high heat. Once hot, add the onions and garlic and cook until translucent, about 3 minutes. Add the tomato paste, honey, and barbecue sauce, stir to combine, and cook for 2 minutes more. Remove from the heat and let cool slightly. Transfer to a blender and purée until smooth.

Place the onion purée, lentils, beef, eggs, mustard, and salt in a large mixing bowl. Mix well (hands do it best!) until everything is incorporated. Transfer the meatloaf mixture to the prepared loaf pan and bake for 45 minutes, brushing the top of the meatloaf with the glaze at the 15- and 30-minute marks.

After 45 minutes, brush the meatloaf with glaze one more time, increase the oven temperature to 400°F, and continue to cook for 15 minutes more. Let cool slightly before slicing and serving.

BRAISED LAMB NECK WITH WHITE BEANS

SERVES 4

TC: The meat found in the neck has a good amount of fat in the muscle and requires a low and slow method of cooking. The process is definitely worth the wait because with braising, you not only release all that fat-enhanced flavour, you also get ridiculously tender meat, loads of rich gravy, and beans so tender they melt in your mouth. Make sure to have a chunk of crusty bread on hand to sop up all the saucy bits. If you can get your hands on lamb, beef, or pork neck, grab it and get braising. Throw a log on the fire, pour a glass of red wine, and get ready for some serious comfort food.

2½ lb lamb neck pieces (see note)

¾ cup all-purpose flour seasoned with salt and pepper

3 Tbsp canola oil

1 medium onion, diced

3 carrots, peeled and diced

3 celery stalks, diced

1 fennel bulb, diced

3 cloves garlic, minced

1 lb dried white beans, soaked for at least 8 hours and drained

1 tsp sea salt

1 tsp freshly ground black pepper

3 sprigs fresh thyme

3 sprigs fresh rosemary or 1 Tbsp dried

1 bay leaf

4 cups chicken broth

Preheat the oven to 325°F.

Pat the pieces of lamb neck dry using paper towel. Dredge the pieces in the seasoned flour and set aside.

Heat the oil in a large (9-quart) Dutch oven over medium-high. Add the lamb in batches and brown until each piece is a nice golden brown colour, 3–4 minutes per side. Place the browned meat in a shallow dish to catch the juices.

Turn the heat to medium and add the onion, carrots, celery, fennel, and garlic to the rendered lamb fat in the pot. Sauté for a few minutes, stirring frequently. Add the beans and stir to combine with the vegetables. Season with the salt and pepper, and add the thyme, rosemary, and bay leaf. Give everything a good stir. Add the lamb pieces back to the pot, pour in chicken broth, cover with a lid, and set in the oven.

Braise for at least 3 hours. The meat should be fall-off-the-bone tender. If the beans are still tough, remove the meat and set aside in a dish, cover to keep warm, and cook the beans for another 30 minutes or until tender.

When serving, season with additional salt and pepper to taste. To store leftovers, place all the ingredients in one lidded container and keep in the fridge for up to 1 week.

NOTE: *Lamb neck is usually found at independent butcher shops and grocery stores—places where a trained butcher is on hand. The packages usually contain four pieces and weigh 2–3 lb. If the neck has been left whole, ask the butcher to cut it into portions for you. It'll only take a minute.*

SASKATCHEWAN BISON STEW

SERVES 5–6

DC: A simple stick-to-your-ribs stew is the perfect thing to cozy up to in the midst of a Prairie winter. Saskatchewan chef Jenni Lessard pulls from fond memories of days gone by when she creates this bison stew for her loved ones.

"When I nourish myself with bison, I feel connected to the land and my relatives past and present. This stew reminds me of cozy meals at my grandmother's house in Prince Albert, Saskatchewan. She'd have the table laid with a blue-and-white checkered tablecloth, and we were encouraged to 'eat up.' I love the smoky flavour imparted by the jerky in this recipe!" —Chef Jenni Lessard, owner of Inspired by Nature Culinary Consulting

¼ cup canola oil or melted lard

¼ cup all-purpose flour

2 tsp salt, divided

½ tsp ground black pepper

1 tsp ground dried sage or 1 Tbsp finely chopped fresh sage

2–2½ lb bison roast, cut into 1-inch cubes

¼ cup finely chopped bison jerky or dried bison meat

1 yellow onion, diced

2 stalks celery, diced

4 parsnips, peeled and sliced into ½-inch rounds

4 carrots, peeled and sliced into ½-inch rounds

6 medium red potatoes, peeled and coarsely chopped

1 can (19 oz) diced tomatoes

2 cups hot, good-quality beef broth

Preheat the oven to 375°F.

Heat the oil in a large non-stick pan over medium-high heat.

Combine the flour, 1 tsp of the salt, pepper, and sage in a medium bowl and toss the bison into the flour mixture to coat. Working in two batches, brown the floured bison on all sides in the pan.

Transfer the browned meat to a large roaster or deep baking dish along with the bison jerky, onion, celery, parsnips, carrots, potatoes, tomatoes, the remaining 1 tsp salt, and the broth. Cover with a lid or tinfoil and bake for 90 minutes. Check the dish at the 45-minute mark and add a little more broth or hot water to the roasting pan if most of the liquid has evaporated. After 90 minutes, the bison meat should be tender and easily broken apart with a fork. Season to taste with additional salt before serving.

MRS. P'S PEROGIES

MAKES 6 DOZEN

TC: Despite perogies appearing to be a simple food, the act of perogy making is rife with nuance. When you first start out, your patience may be sorely tried. Don't give up. Keep going until you get it right. Ultimately, homemade is best by a country mile. The dough recipe here is from my friend's mom, Marge Pasichnuk. I've tried other dough recipes over the years, but this one has never let me down. Mrs. P's dough is always silky soft and easily rolls out without tearing.

These days, almost anything goes when it comes to filling, but I usually stay traditional with cottage cheese and dill, or mashed potato with cooked onion. If you can mash it or put it in a mound (like sauerkraut and bacon), you can use it for filling. As far as toppings go, onions sautéed in butter finished with a dollop of sour cream on top are standard.

Cottage Cheese and Dill Filling

2 cups dry cottage cheese

2 Tbsp thinly sliced green onion

3 Tbsp chopped fresh dill

1 egg

¾ tsp salt

¼ tsp black pepper

Perogy Dough

5 cups all-purpose flour

1½ tsp salt

½ cup canola oil

1¾ cups hot tap water

Cottage Cheese and Dill Filling

To a medium bowl, add the cottage cheese, green onion, dill, egg, salt, and pepper. Use a spoon to mix all the ingredients until well combined. Set aside until ready to use.

Perogy Dough

Sift the flour into a large bowl. Add the salt and oil to the flour and stir to combine. The mixture will appear dry, and that's okay. Slowly add the water while stirring to incorporate into the other ingredients. All the liquid should be incorporated into the mixture, resulting in a loose dough that is sticky but cohesive.

Rub some flour on your hands and knead the dough on a floured surface until you have a fairly smooth round ball. Place the dough back in the bowl, cover with a damp clean dish towel, and let rest for 30 minutes at room temperature.

continued on next page

Butter and Onion Topping (for
　1 Dozen Perogies)

¾ cup butter

1 large onion, chopped

2 Tbsp chopped fresh chives

½ cup sour cream (optional), for
　serving

Butter and Onion Topping (for 1 Dozen Perogies)

While the dough is resting, melt the butter in a medium saucepan. Add the onion and cook for about 10 minutes, until soft. Stir the onions and lower the heat if necessary to prevent them from browning. Cover and set aside.

Sprinkle some flour onto a clean work surface and turn out the rested dough onto the surface. To make things more manageable, cut the dough ball in half and work with one portion. Return the other portion to the bowl, covered with the damp towel so it doesn't dry out.

Roll the dough to the point where it's thin but won't tear, about $1/16$ inch thick. (This is the step that you'll get better at each time you make perogies. You'll get to know when the dough is "thin enough.")

Use a glass or cookie cutter about 3 inches wide to cut out circles of dough.

Add about $1\frac{1}{2}$ tsp of filling to the middle of each round and gather the edges up to pinch together. (If you get filling on the edges, your dough won't hold together when you put the perogies in the water to cook, so be careful.)

Bring a large pot of salted water to a medium boil. If the water boils too rapidly, it could tear the dumplings.

When the water reaches a boil, add 10–12 perogies at a time to cook. Stir immediately so they don't stick to the bottom of the pot. Let them flutter to the top and float there for about 5 minutes before removing with a slotted spoon. Place them on a platter, top with the melted butter and onion, and sprinkle with fresh dill. Serve with sour cream on the side.

Alternatively, you can fry the perogies after they've been boiled. In this case, melt 3 Tbsp of butter in a large frying pan over medium heat, add the perogies, and fry until golden, about 3 minutes per side. Place on a platter, spoon butter and onions over top, sprinkle with fresh chives, and serve with sour cream.

To Freeze Uncooked Perogies

Sprinkle flour on a baking sheet and place the perogies in rows. If further layers are needed, place parchment paper between each layer. Cover the entire sheet with a large plastic bag and place in the freezer. Once the perogies are frozen, package them in a large zip-lock bag or sealable plastic container and keep them in the freezer for up to 6 months.

To Cook from Frozen

Bring a large pot of salted water to a medium boil. Add no more than 12 perogies at a time, stirring for about 30 seconds to keep them from sticking to the bottom of the pot. Cook for approximately 10 minutes, and when they float to the top, let them stay there for a minute more before removing them with a slotted spoon. Place them on a platter and top with the melted butter, onions, and chives.

BLACK GARLIC CHOCOLATE CHIP COOKIES

MAKES 36 COOKIES

TC: Want to wow members of your Christmas cookie-swap group in December? Give them a batch of these wickedly delicious morsels. As it happens, black garlic and chocolate play very well together. This recipe comes courtesy of Kristin Graves of Fifth Gen Gardens in central Alberta. Among the plethora of gorgeous ingredients that Kristin grows, many of which are sourced by chefs, her garlic is top tier.

This recipe is a fun take on a childhood favourite, she says. "As a garlic farmer, I wanted to create something that would showcase the uniqueness of local ingredients. While my mom would fold in cherries, I've opted to add black garlic, a product we make ourselves here on the farm. The beauty of this recipe is that it's a real conversation starter. Everyone knows that garlic can be overpowering, but when garlic is kept at low heat over a period of weeks, it ferments and the flavour becomes subtle and surprisingly sweet." —Kristin Graves, Fifth Gen Gardens

1¼ cups all-purpose flour

½ tsp salt

½ tsp baking soda

½ cup butter, at room temperature

½ cup granulated sugar

¼ cup packed brown sugar

1 egg

1 cup semi-sweet chocolate chips

3 Tbsp (about 2 bulbs) black garlic, peeled and cut into small pieces

Preheat the oven to 375°F.

To a small bowl, add the flour, salt, and baking soda. Mix and set aside.

In a medium bowl, cream together the butter, granulated sugar, brown sugar, and egg. Stir in the chocolate chips and black garlic. Add the flour mixture and mix until combined.

Mix the dough further using your hands and roll it into ping-pong-sized balls. Place on two ungreased baking sheets, about 1 inch apart.

Bake for 8–10 minutes. Allow to cool for 30 seconds before removing from the baking sheets. Allow to cool completely, about 30 minutes, and store in a lidded, airtight container for up to 1 week.

PRAIRIE WINTER WONDERLAND LAYER CAKE

MAKES ONE 14-INCH LAYER CAKE (SERVES 8-10)

DC: As a former owner of one of the top bakeshops in the Prairies, Winnipeg's Pam Kirkpatrick works wonders with cakes and cupcakes. The baker-turned-front-of-house-manager was an integral part of my inaugural Prairie Grid Dinner Series in 2017. The menu for that first roving pop-up concept drew inspiration from the prairie landscape—how the farmland looks from a bird's-eye view, the array of colours that changes with each season, and even the snow-covered ground and the layers of earth beneath. Snow and frozen earth were Pam's inspiration for this cake. It's a whimsical reminder that even in the dead of winter, there is beauty to be found in the Prairies.

"For the Prairie Grid Dinner Series, we wanted the cakes to look like the earth when cut through with the guests' forks. We made little individual cakes for the guests, but at home you could present the cake whole and cut slices for your people. Either way, it's all about the layers here." —**Pam Kirkpatrick, general manager at Bonnie Day**

Chocolate Cake

¾ cup all-purpose flour, plus more for pans

2 cups granulated sugar

¾ cup good cocoa powder

2 tsp baking soda

1 tsp baking powder

1 tsp kosher salt

1 cup plain yogurt

½ cup canola oil

2 eggs, at room temperature

1 tsp pure vanilla extract

1 cup freshly brewed, good-quality hot coffee

Cinnamon Sugared Nuts

1 egg white

1 Tbsp water

Chocolate Cake

Preheat the oven to 350°F. Butter and flour two 8-inch round cake pans, or line with parchment paper.

Place the flour, sugar, cocoa, baking soda, baking powder, and salt in the bowl of a stand mixer with the paddle attachment. Mix on low speed for 30 seconds, until combined.

In another medium bowl, stir to combine the yogurt, oil, eggs, and vanilla. With the mixer on low speed, slowly add the wet ingredients to the dry until incorporated. Add the coffee and continue to mix on low speed until just combined, scraping the bottom of the bowl with a rubber spatula.

Pour the batter into the prepared pans and bake for 35–40 minutes. Check with a toothpick and keep baking in 7–10 minute intervals if necessary until it comes out clean when inserted into the centre. Cool the cakes in the pans for

½ cup granulated sugar

¼ cup packed brown sugar

2 tsp cinnamon

2 cups raw hazelnuts

1 cup raw sunflower seeds

Classic Vanilla Buttercream Icing

1 cup butter, at room temperature

4 cups icing sugar

¼ cup heavy (35%) cream

2 tsp vanilla

2 tsp cocoa powder

1 pinch salt

Easy Fluffy Whip

2 cups heavy (35%) cream

1 cup icing sugar

2 tsp pure vanilla

1 pinch salt

30 minutes, then turn them out onto a cooling rack and allow to cool completely. Turn the oven temperature down to 300°F for the cinnamon sugared nuts. If you're using these cake layers the next day, wrap them in plastic wrap and leave at room temperature overnight. You can also freeze the cakes at this point as well, wrapping with a couple more layers of plastic wrap to keep them from getting frosty. If you do freeze the cakes, they will last for up to 2 weeks. As well, leave them wrapped and thaw for a couple of hours on the counter before cake assembly.

Cinnamon Sugared Nuts

Line a baking sheet with parchment paper.

In a small bowl, whisk together the egg white and water until frothy, about 2 minutes. Set aside.

Place the granulated sugar, brown sugar, and cinnamon in a medium bowl and stir to combine. In a large bowl, mix the hazelnuts, sunflower seeds, and egg white mixture until well combined. Stir in the sugar mixture to evenly coat.

Spread the nuts evenly onto the prepared baking sheet. Bake for 25–30 minutes, until lightly browned and toasted, stirring every 10 minutes or so.

When cooling the nuts on the pan on the counter, break the mixture apart with a spoon. Once cooled, coarsely chop the nuts and set aside.

Classic Vanilla Buttercream Icing

In the bowl of a stand mixer, cream the butter, pushing down any butter on the sides of the stand mixer bowl with a spatula. Slowly add in the icing sugar in ½ cup intervals, continuing to clean the sides of the bowl with a spatula as necessary.

continued on next page

Add the cream, vanilla, cocoa, and salt. Mix the ingredients in, then whip on high for 30 seconds to incorporate fully. The icing should be firm enough to hold soft peaks.

Easy Fluffy Whip

Using an electric hand-held mixer, a stand mixer, or a whisk and your own arm (you can do it!), whisk the cream until it begins to thicken. Slowly mix in the icing sugar, vanilla, and salt, and then whip on high, or as fast as you can, just until you get to firm peaks. Do not overmix. You can always stop and mix a little more if needed, but you cannot unmix if you turn it to butter. Use immediately to assemble the cake.

Place one of the chocolate cake layers on a cake plate and slather a generous amount of buttercream icing overtop, approximately 1¼ cups. Next, add a layer of the candied nuts, and top with the other layer of cake.

With the remaining buttercream icing, apply a thin layer of icing over the entirety of the cake—both the sides and top. It is A-okay if your icing picks up the cake crumbs, as it will add a soil-like visual to the layers.

Chill the cake for 45–60 minutes before covering with the easy fluffy whip, so that the whip stays white and clean. The whip is meant to resemble drifting snow, so after you have covered the top and sides of the cake with the whip, use a spoon to add big swoops to get that side-of-the-prairie-highway-snow-drift effect.

Any leftovers can be stored in a sealed container in the fridge for up to 1 week.

THE PRAIRIE CARIBOU DRINK

SERVES 6–8

DC: I know what many of you are thinking: Why is Dan putting a majestic animal in a cocktail? This drink is hyper-seasonal to Winnipeggers and is almost exclusively available during the city's annual Festival du Voyageur. Each year, the epic 10-day winter festival takes place in February and highlights a wide array of creative folks, be they cooks serving up French-Canadian cuisine, ice sculptors from around the globe, Canadian musicians, and more. It is a total blast and should be on every Canadian's bucket list for winter events to experience.

But I digress . . . At its simplest, Caribou is a fortified wine—a red wine enhanced by whisky and maple syrup, and it is commercially produced in Quebec. My version pays respectful homage, but opts for a currant wine and some Crown Royal (bet you didn't know this rye giant is actually based in Gimli, Manitoba!), among other Prairie-grown ingredients. Feel free to serve this one hot or cold. Either way you'll be feeling cozy after a few sips.

1 bottle (750 mL) Living Sky Winery currant wine (or similar fruit wine)

1 cup rye whisky (I like Crown Royal Northern Harvest Rye)

¼ cup pure maple syrup

¼ cup dried Saskatoon berries

2 tsp dried rosehips (see note on page 272)

1 cinnamon stick (optional)

Place all ingredients in a medium pot and bring to a near-simmer over medium heat. Once steaming, but not bubbling, reduce the heat to low, cover, and keep on low heat for 20 minutes to allow the flavours to mingle.

Ladle into heat-safe glasses or mugs and enjoy.

WINTER-SPICED PRAIRIE CREAM WHISKY

MAKES 3¼ CUPS

DC: Give me *all* the winter spices when it's chilly out. All of them! Cream whiskies have risen in popularity steadily over the past few years, but it wasn't that long ago that Baileys dominated the market. These days, we've got plenty of options from coast to coast . . . but it always tastes best when you make it yourself. Making winter-spiced cream whisky has become a holiday season tradition for me and many of my friends. You can whip up a batch of this smooth, warming, and appropriately boozy stuff in no time, making it perfect for portioning out and gifting to party hosts, colleagues, friends, and more. Trust me when I say this is one of the easiest gifts you could ever make for someone. Ever. Gift it to yourself too, of course, by way of a splash or two in your morning coffee. You deserve it.

1¼ cups good-quality rye whisky (I use Alberta Premium Whisky)

1 cup heavy (35%) cream

1 can (14 oz) sweetened condensed milk

1 Tbsp instant coffee

1 Tbsp cocoa powder

1 Tbsp liquid honey

1 tsp pure vanilla extract

½ tsp ground cinnamon

¼ tsp ground tonka bean (optional)

¼ tsp ground cloves

1 pinch nutmeg

Place all of the ingredients in a blender and blend on medium speed for 20–30 seconds.

Pour the cream whisky into a large container, bottle, or mason jar, seal, and store in the fridge. It will keep slightly longer than the expiry date on the cream you used to create it.

NOTE: *This recipe is easily adaptable when it comes to suggested spices. Don't like cloves? Leave 'em out! Think it could use a little ground ginger? Why not? Any spice that would feel at home in a pumpkin pie would fit the bill here.*

There is no shortage of top-tier whiskies and rye whiskies available across the Prairies, many of which are based in Alberta. Here's a list of spirits that would be ideal to create this winter-spiced cream whisky:

- PARK Distillery's Maple Rye (Banff)
- Burwood Distillery's Single Hive Bourbon (Calgary)
- Hansen Distillery's Northern Eyes Whisky (Edmonton)
- Black Fox Farm and Distillery's SE Eleven Canadian Whisky (Saskatoon)
- Crown Royal Northern Harvest Rye (Winkler, Manitoba)

SPRING

WHEN IT COMES TO COOKING,

spring is a cruel mistress. With the snow melting away, temperatures climbing to non-toque-and-mitts-needed levels and the sun lingering in the sky longer than in the past few months, one starts to crave fresher flavours–often lighter eats too. But although the snow may be gone, the ground in the Prairies stays frozen well into April. That means we're not seeing any budding (edible) greens outdoors–let alone any locally grown produce–until peak summer.

It's not all bad, though. You can still get your hands on a now-dwindling supply of cellared fruits like pears and apples–yes, you can find plenty of these grown in the Prairies–as well as plenty of root vegetables. We'd be remiss to not mention the proliferation of green-house agriculture and hydroponics in the Prairies, both of which allow a person to enjoy healthy greens and vegetables like tomatoes, cucumbers, and most recently even strawberries out of season.

Of all four seasons, spring throws the most curveballs to us home cooks when it comes to having our food match the weather. It can be 20°C on April 1 (no joke!) and then back down to near-zero for an unexpected blizzard come the May long weekend (also no joke!). That means you need recipes that can deliver everything from a big, cozy bowl of soup to a main dish that would feel fitting on a midsummer's night. Here's how we like to make the most of everyone's least favourite season, spring.

ASPARAGUS, WILD MUSHROOM, AND MIXED HERB ORZO SALAD

SERVES 4

TC: When asparagus and peas are picked at the height of the season, the best way to enjoy their sweet herbaceous flavour is to eat them raw. Combine them with mushrooms and salty feta, a handful of fresh herbs, and cooked pasta to make a salad that's both refreshing and filling.

2 cups orzo

1 Tbsp butter

½ lb wild mushroom mix

½ tsp salt

Freshly ground black pepper

½ lb asparagus

1 cup fresh peas

1 cup crumbled feta

1 handful fresh herbs (flat-leaf parsley, cilantro, and basil), coarsely chopped

2 Tbsp minced fresh chives

½ cup Apple Cider Vinaigrette (page 269)

Cook the orzo according to the package directions.

While the pasta is cooking, set a medium non-stick skillet over medium heat. Add the butter and heat it until it has melted and starts to foam. Add the mushrooms and season with the salt and a few grinds of pepper. Fry the mushrooms, stirring occasionally, until lightly golden.

Snap off the bottoms—the last inch or so—of the asparagus spears and discard. Cut the spears into 1-inch pieces and place in a large bowl. Add the cooked mushrooms, peas, feta, orzo, herbs, and chives. Pour the vinaigrette over the salad and toss to coat.

BACON-WRAPPED ASPARAGUS
WITH SEA BUCKTHORN AIOLI

SERVES 6

TC: Spring asparagus is awesome simply washed and nibbled on like a carrot stalk, but giving it a little bacon love isn't such a bad way to go, either. Serving it enrobed in crispy bacon lets asparagus act more like the centrepiece that it deserves to be, rather than a runner-up side component. This dish gets even more star treatment with a condiment of vibrant Sea Buckthorn Aioli (see page 261). In one bite you get salt, fat, earthiness, and a bit of zip. Have these savoury spears with afternoon beers on the deck or serve them alongside Chef Garrett Martin's Spinach Dumplings (page 225) for a full meal.

1 bundle asparagus (about 1½ lb)

1 lb bacon

½ cup Sea Buckthorn Aioli (page 261)

Preheat the oven to 400°F and line a baking sheet with a silicone liner or parchment paper.

Snap off the woody ends of the asparagus and set aside. (To find the right spot, apply gentle pressure up from the bottom of the stalk until it snaps. It's typically 1½ –2 inches from the bottom.)

Place the bacon on a cutting board and cut the strips in half so that they are about 5 inches long. Wrap the bacon around each stalk of asparagus and place on the prepared baking sheet.

Bake for 15 minutes or until the bacon is dark brown and crispy, turning once at the halfway mark.

When the bacon-asparagus spears are cooked, use tongs to place them on a platter. Place the aioli alongside and eat the spears while they're warm. These do not reheat well, so enjoy them while they're fresh!

HERBED GREEN SPLIT PEAS AND ASPARAGUS ON TOAST

SERVES 4

DC: When was the last time you enjoyed split peas in a presentation other than soup? While I truly live for a split pea and ham soup on a chilly winter's day—I have fond memories of my mom making big batches of it for us to enjoy for dinner, followed by lunch the next day along with some soda bread—once I'm out of hibernation, I look at them in a new light.

Learning about agricultural processes over the years in my food-writing work, I've come to know that split peas are grown all across Alberta. Finding a bag of Prairie split peas at your local grocery store is pretty darn easy regardless of whether you're in Western Canada, out east, or even outside of Canada.

It's helpful, you know, having something green that you can eat in the springtime when fresh peas are still a month or two out of reach. This toast celebrates the wonderful texture of al dente split peas coupled with spring vegetables like spinach and asparagus, fresh herbs, a little kick courtesy of an amazing Calgary-made hot sauce, and a slathering of labneh for some added brightness.

Herbed Green Split Peas

1 cup dried green split peas, rinsed

3 cups vegetable broth

¼ cup good-quality pickle brine

1 cup lightly packed fresh herbs (I use a mix of basil, parsley, mint, and tarragon, but use what you enjoy)

¼ cup cold-pressed canola oil

Salt

Herbed Green Split Peas

Place the dried peas, broth, and pickle brine in a medium pot and bring to a boil over medium-high heat. Reduce the heat to medium and simmer until the peas have a slightly al dente texture, approximately 25 minutes. Do not allow the peas to go mushy; you want the end product to have a bit of a bite.

Strain the peas in a colander, reserving approximately ¼ cup of the cooking liquid. Place the cooked peas and liquid in a food processor along with the fresh herbs and pulse while slowly adding the oil until a chunky paste forms. Season to taste with salt and set aside to cool to room temperature.

continued on next page

Asparagus and Spinach Salad

6 asparagus spears, thinly cut on the diagonal

1 cup lightly packed thinly sliced spinach

1 Tbsp flaxseed oil

2 tsp Knockout Heat Co. Serrano Vinegar (or comparable pepper-infused vinegar)

¼ tsp salt

Assembly

½–⅔ cup labneh, enough to cover 6 pieces of toast (I use Chaeban Artisan labneh)

6 pieces sourdough or locally made Italian-style white bread, toasted

Salt

Asparagus and Spinach Salad

Place the asparagus, spinach, oil, vinegar, and salt in a medium bowl and toss to combine. Let sit for a few minutes (the spinach will wilt notably), toss again, and set aside until ready to assemble the toast.

Assembly

Slather a healthy layer of labneh onto each piece of toasted bread. Top with approximately 2 Tbsp of the green split pea and herb mixture, followed by a dollop of the asparagus and spinach salad. Season lightly with salt and serve immediately.

NOTE: *If you toss a fried egg on top of this dish, you've got yourself a pretty lovely spring brunch dish too. Just saying . . .*

SEARED HALLOUMI WITH HASKAP AND CARAMELIZED ONION JAM

SERVES 2-3

DC: If it were socially acceptable to eat halloumi for breakfast, lunch, and dinner, I would do so happily. I mean, it's not as if I can't do that, but it may not be the healthiest choice to make. Regardless of the time of day, searing (or grilling) this firm, salty cheese of Greek descent never gets old for me. The magic it possesses to hold its structure at high temperatures leads to crispy-on-the-outside and still-squishy-on-the-inside results. Here, I fancy it up a tad by adding dollops of a vibrant-coloured haskap and onion jam that is an idyllic example of sweet and savoury, and a finishing of cold-pressed canola oil. If you're looking for a simple but visually impressive cheese course at your next dinner party, this is it.

Haskap and Caramelized Onion Jam

2 Tbsp canola oil

4 yellow onions, halved and thinly sliced

2½ cups fresh or frozen haskap berries

2 Tbsp butter

2 Tbsp honey

1 tsp salt

2 Tbsp haskap gin (Black Fox Farm and Distillery or Fort Distillery products are great options)

Haskap and Caramelized Onion Jam

Heat the oil in a large non-stick pan over medium-high heat. Add the onions and cook, stirring occasionally, until they are soft and translucent, 4–5 minutes.

Reduce the heat to medium and continue to cook for 20 minutes, stirring occasionally, or until the onions turn a deep golden colour.

If brown bits begin to form on pieces of the onion or the bottom of the pan, add splashes of water to help deglaze. Repeat this process as necessary.

Once the onions have caramelized, add the haskap berries, butter, honey, salt, and gin and let simmer for 15 minutes uncovered. The berries should break down and the mixture should thicken noticeably.

Transfer to a food processor or blender and purée to a smooth consistency.

continued on next page

Assembly

1 Tbsp canola oil

1 package (9 oz) halloumi, sliced crosswise into 8–10 equal pieces

Cold-pressed canola oil, for coating the serving plate, approximately ¼ cup

Salt

Assembly

Place the oil and cheese slices in a medium bowl and toss until evenly coated.

Heat a large non-stick pan over medium-high heat. Once hot, place the cheese slices in the pan, leaving approximately 1 inch of space between pieces. Cook until golden brown on each side, about 2 minutes per side. Transfer to paper towel to absorb excess oil before assembling.

Pour enough cold-pressed canola oil onto a serving plate so that a thin layer of oil covers the entire plate. Spread out dollops of the haskap and onion jam on the plate, top with the halloumi slices, and season lightly with salt before serving.

CHEESY PEPPERONI PRETZEL BAKE

SERVES 3-4

DC: Did you know that the best pretzels in the country can be found in Edmonton? I say this with much certainty—Zwick's Pretzels has the Midas touch when it comes to their baking. The problem with such delicious pretzels, though, is that I wind up taking home too many. Whenever I have leftovers, I love to take a page out of my friend D'orjay's book (figuratively) and use them in a pretzel bake. Think of this as the love child of a savoury bread pudding, a pepperoni pizza, and a pretzel. What a love triangle!

The nice thing about this dish is that there really isn't a bad time to enjoy it. Lovely at a weekend brunch served with some soft scrambled eggs on the side, a nice complement to pasta (think garlic bread alternative), after midnight when you need some satisfying munchies. And . . . well, you get the point.

¼ cup half and half cream

2 large eggs

5 cups hand-torn day-old pretzels

½ cup thinly sliced good-quality salami (I like Saltcraft Meat Co.'s fennel salami)

1 cup + 1 Tbsp finely grated parmesan cheese, divided

¼ cup seeded, thinly sliced pepperoncini peppers, patted dry

½ cup + 2 Tbsp tomato sauce, divided

Salt

1 cup shredded good-quality mozzarella

Preheat the oven to 400°F. Grease a 5 × 9-inch loaf pan.

Whisk together the cream and eggs in a medium bowl.

Place the pretzels, salami, 1 cup of the parmesan cheese, the peppers, and ½ cup of the tomato sauce into a large mixing bowl. Pour in the egg mixture and stir well to combine.

Place half the mixture into the prepared loaf pan, followed by the mozzarella. Top with the remaining pretzel mixture, then dot with the remaining 2 Tbsp tomato sauce and then sprinkle the remaining 1 Tbsp of parmesan evenly across the top. Bake until golden brown and bubbly, about 25 minutes. Season with the salt to taste and let cool slightly before serving.

CHORIZO AND APPLES

SERVES 2–3

DC: Winnipeg may not be the first city that comes to mind when thinking of Spanish cuisine, but the now-closed Segovia consistently cooked up creative and refined tapas-inspired dishes with global flavours. After closing during the first wave of the pandemic in 2020, it is very much missed by locals and tourists alike. Celebrated chef and Prairie Grid Dinner Series alumnus Adam Donnelly shares how to make this delicious signature dish from his former restaurant at home. It's a simple tapa that comes together in no time and always hits the spot. Serve it alongside a smattering of marinated olives, bread, and cheese . . . and maybe even a glass of cava too.

"I've always loved Spanish-style cooking and creating small tapas that people can share with one another. This recipe is a great opportunity to incorporate locally cured meats and cider into your cooking. If you've got an apple tree in your backyard, then use some of those too." —Adam Donnelly, chef and owner of Winnipeg's Petit Socco

6 oz dry-cured chorizo, cut into ¼-inch-thick slices (I like Empire Provisions' chorizo out of Calgary)

1 gala apple, cored and diced

1 bay leaf

1 Tbsp Alchemist Vinegar Honey Blackened Garlic Vinegar (or good-quality wine vinegar)

1 Tbsp honey

6 Tbsp hard medium-dry apple cider (I like Dead Horse Cider Company's Bright Cider)

Dried oregano

Dried chili flakes

Maldon sea salt

Cook the chorizo in a dry non-stick pan over medium-high heat for 3–4 minutes to render out some of the fat. Add the apple and cook for another couple of minutes. Add the bay leaf, vinegar, and honey. Cook, stirring occasionally, until the mixture completely glazes the chorizo and apples, 2–3 minutes.

Pour in the cider and continue to cook until the cider reduces by about three-quarters. (The liquid should be thick, and you should now have a nice sweet glaze on the chorizo and apples.) Season to taste with the oregano, chili flakes, and salt. Stir well and transfer to a serving dish. Serve immediately.

HEMP, LENTIL, AND SUNFLOWER SEED CRACKERS

MAKES 2 DOZEN CRACKERS

DC: As much as I go on and on about not being able to bake, what I *can* "bake" successfully is seed crackers. Both more delicious and much more economical than the seed crackers you'll find at the grocery store, my recipe also succeeds at celebrating three major Prairie crops: Alberta's sunflower seeds, Saskatchewan's lentils, and Manitoba's hemp hearts. You'll notice below that I call for Chef Scott Redekopp's Prairie Grid Spice Blend (page 270) as well. If you're not up for making a batch (it's easy, though, I promise), then substitute everything bagel seasoning or some dehydrated onions.

2 egg whites

3 Tbsp water

1 Tbsp maple syrup

1 Tbsp canola oil

½ tsp salt

⅓ cup + 1 Tbsp dried red lentils

⅔ cup raw sunflower seeds

⅔ cup hemp hearts

1 tsp Prairie Grid Spice Blend
  (page 270)

Preheat the oven to 350°F. Line a baking sheet with parchment paper.

Place the egg whites, water, maple syrup, oil, and salt in a medium bowl and whisk vigorously until the mixture becomes frothy, 20–30 seconds.

Blitz the lentils quickly in a blender or food processor until coarsely ground.

Add the lentils, sunflower seeds, hemp hearts, and seasoning to the egg white mixture. Stir well and let sit for 10 minutes to allow the seed mixture to absorb the majority of the liquid. Transfer the mixture to the prepared baking sheet. Place a piece of greased parchment paper on top and press the mixture by hand as flat as possible before baking. Discard the top piece of parchment once you are done pressing.

Bake for 25 minutes, then reduce the temperature to 300°F and continue to cook until the cracker mixture is brown and crispy, about 20 minutes more. Cool completely in the baking sheet before breaking up into about 2 dozen crackers. These will keep in an airtight container at room temperature for up to 2 weeks.

SMOKED GOLDEYE AND CARAMELIZED ONION DIP

SERVES 3–4

DC: Saskatchewan loves pike, Albertans are on the trout train, but Manitoba? It loves its goldeye. This fish is at its best when it's smoked and that's the way you'll find it at most spots in Winnipeg. Two Hands chef and co-owner Michael Robins first introduced me to this delicious smoked fish during our Prairie Grid Dinner Series in 2018, and I've been a big fan ever since. This dip recipe, adapted from Robins' restaurant version, is especially rewarding in the early spring when all you've got (that's local) are a few cellared vegetables, such as onions.

"If you live out of the province and can't get your hands on smoked goldeye, then a good-quality smoked fish in your region should do just fine." —Michael Robins, chef and co-owner of Two Hands.

2 Tbsp canola oil

2 yellow onions, diced

13 oz cream cheese, softened

⅓ cup sour cream

⅓ cup mayonnaise

2 tsp minced garlic

1 tsp Worcestershire sauce

1 Tbsp finely chopped fresh flat-leaf parsley

4 dashes hot sauce of choice (I like Tasty Heat's Sunny hot sauce)

2 pinches black pepper

2 pinches salt

2 Tbsp apple cider vinegar

1 Tbsp smoked sweet paprika

1 cup + 1 Tbsp smoked goldeye, skin and bones removed, broken into small pieces, divided

1 Tbsp thinly sliced green onions

1 Tbsp coarsely chopped fresh dill

Slices of bread or crackers, for dipping

Heat the oil in a large pan over medium heat. Add the onions and cook, stirring occasionally, until they are caramelized and golden brown, about 25 minutes. (If brown bits begin to form at the bottom of the pan during the caramelization process, add small splashes of water to help deglaze. Repeat as necessary.) Set aside to cool.

Once the onions have cooled, place the cream cheese, sour cream, mayonnaise, garlic, Worcestershire sauce, parsley, hot sauce, pepper, salt, vinegar, paprika, and 1 cup of the smoked goldeye in a large bowl and stir until thoroughly combined.

To serve, place the dip in a serving bowl and top with the remaining 1 Tbsp smoked goldeye, green onions, and dill. Enjoy with your favourite bread or crackers. Will keep in the fridge in a sealed container for up to 1 week.

ROASTED CHEESE CURDS WITH HONEY PEPPER SAUCE

SERVES 4

DC: One of my absolute favourite dishes to eat in the Prairies is Christine Sandford's coal-roasted cheese curds with fermented banana peppers at Biera in Edmonton. Trust me when I say that bubbly melted cheese has never tasted so good. I've drawn inspiration from this ooey-gooey menu item and created a home cook's version using some fantastic local cheese curds (by way of Alberta's Lakeside Farmstead) and plenty of pickled peppers to balance out the richness. It's the perfect pick-me-up in the early spring to distract you from the dull hues of brown and grey outside.

Honey Pepper Sauce

2 Tbsp chopped pickled jalapeños

2 Tbsp chopped banana peppers

1 Tbsp pickled jalapeño brine

1 Tbsp banana pepper brine

4 Tbsp canola oil

1 Tbsp grainy mustard

1 Tbsp honey

Salt

Assembly

2 cups good-quality local cheese curds (we like Lakeside Farmstead's cheese)

Hand-Torn Garlic Bread (page 263)

Honey Pepper Sauce

Place the jalapeños, banana peppers, pickled jalapeño brine, banana pepper brine, canola oil, mustard, and honey in a small bowl and stir to combine. Add salt to taste.

Assembly

Preheat the oven to broil.

Place the cheese curds in a small or medium oven-safe skillet. Broil in the oven until the cheese has melted and the top is brown and bubbly. Remove from the oven and let cool slightly, 4–5 minutes, before serving.

Serve with the garlic bread and honey pepper sauce. Dunk and dollop accordingly!

SMOKED LAKE FISH CHOWDER

SERVES 4

DC: I've had delicious chowders across the country, from Tofino to Halifax, and it is always inspiring to see chefs working with their local, sustainable seafood options to find delicious success. We may not have the diver scallops of the East Coast or the fresh-off-the-shore mussels of Vancouver Island, but trust me when I say that a Prairie lake fish chowder can still hold its own. The somewhat unorthodox and "secret" ingredient in this recipe is beef jerky. Please don't omit it! I'll tell you why: the jerky provides a nice depth of flavour, adds subtle smokiness to this soup, and when it slowly cooks and tenderizes it mimics the texture of bacon.

2 Tbsp sunflower oil

2 yellow onions, diced

4 cloves garlic, coarsely chopped

2 Tbsp butter

4½ cups peeled, diced russet potatoes, divided

4 cups vegetable broth

2 cups water

1 pinch salt, plus more for seasoning

1 cup diced carrots

1 cup diced turnips

½ cup finely chopped beef jerky (I like Meat Chops Grassfed Beef Jerky)

⅓ cup minced sour pickled pearl onions

2 Tbsp pickled onion brine

4½ oz chunk of brie, with the rind (I like Lakeside Farmstead Brie)

1 cup coarsely chopped smoked trout (or other smoked lake fish like pike or goldeye)

Heat the oil in a large pot over medium-high heat. Add the onions and garlic and cook for 5 minutes, stirring occasionally. Add the butter, reduce the heat to medium, and continue to cook for 5 more minutes to allow the onions to deepen in colour.

Add 3 cups of the potatoes, the broth, water, and salt and allow to come to a simmer. Cook until the potatoes are fork-tender, about 12 minutes.

Use an immersion blender to purée the contents of the pot until silky smooth. Add the remaining 1½ cups diced potatoes, the carrots, turnips, beef jerky, pickled onions, and brine to the pot. Return to a simmer and cook, uncovered, for 15 minutes.

Add the brie to the pot. After 2–3 minutes, the interior of the brie will have dissolved completely into the broth, but the rind will still be whole. Remove and discard the rind.

Reduce to the heat to low, gently stir in the smoked trout, and cook for another 5 minutes or so before seasoning to taste with more salt and serving.

SORREL, FARRO, AND CHICKEN SOUP

SERVES 2

TC: Tangy sorrel, a late-spring leafy green, replaces lemon in this Canadian version of the Greek soup avgolemono. I love using farro—an ancient high-fibre wheat strain similar to the very first wheat cultivated by ancient Mediterranean civilizations. It is the perfect stand-in for rice, as it creates the same bulk while delivering a slight toasty flavour. This soup is light but hearty with a tanginess that brightens up those days where the thaw and the heat are slow to come.

½ cup farro, rinsed

1½ cups water

¼ tsp salt

1 Tbsp canola oil

½ cup white onion

1 cup sorrel, finely chopped

2 cups chicken broth

1 egg

½ tsp white vinegar

1 cup coarsely shredded, cooked chicken meat

Salt and pepper

1 tsp cold-pressed canola oil

Add the farro to a small pot with the water and salt. Bring to a boil, cover, and simmer for 30 minutes. The texture should be chewy but tender. When done, fluff the grains and set aside.

Add the oil to a medium pot and heat over medium-low heat. Add the onion and sauté until soft. Add the sorrel and stir for about 3 minutes, until wilted.

Add the cooked farro and broth. Bring to a boil, then reduce the heat to low and simmer for 15 minutes. Remove the pot from the heat and partially blend the soup with an immersion blender. Return the pot to the stove and bring the soup back to a simmer.

Crack the egg into the mixture and stir for 30 seconds. Add the vinegar and chicken, and season with salt and pepper. Heat through and serve, finished with a drizzle of cold-pressed canola oil on top.

MUSHROOMS
WITH MORNAY SAUCE

SERVES 4

DC: Trust me when I say that Saskatoon's Hearth Restaurant takes mushrooms on toast to a whole new level. Its co-owners and co-chefs (and Prairie Grid Dinner Series 2018 alumni) Beth Rogers and Thayne Robstad have an unabashed love of creating elevated comfort food with local ingredients, and it is this authenticity that has cemented them as two of the best chefs in the Prairies. Their famed mushroom dish is created using locally cultivated or foraged mushrooms with a bubbling-hot Mornay sauce and toast points.

"At the restaurant we garnish the top of this dish with pickled chanterelles and foraged reindeer moss. It's pretty *and* delicious! You might not be able to readily find reindeer moss where you're located, but make sure to scope out your local farmers' market to see what fungi are up for grabs." —Beth Rogers, co-owner and co-chef of Hearth Restaurant

Mornay Sauce

2 cups homogenized milk

3 Tbsp butter

⅓ cup all-purpose flour

3½ oz grated aged white cheddar

5 Tbsp buttermilk

1 pinch nutmeg

Salt

Mushroom Sauté

18 oz cleaned mushrooms, uniformly sliced (we like a mix of button mushrooms, oyster mushrooms, and rehydrated morels)

2 Tbsp butter, divided

1 clove garlic, minced

¼ cup white wine

2 Tbsp finely chopped fresh flat-leaf parsley

Salt

Mornay Sauce

Heat the milk in a small pot over medium-high heat until just before boiling and set aside.

In a medium pot, melt the butter. Add the flour, whisking to form a roux. Slowly add the hot milk to the roux while whisking. While whisking continuously, bring the mixture to a simmer. Once bubbling, remove from the heat and stir in the cheddar until melted. Continue to stir while adding the buttermilk and nutmeg. Season with salt to taste.

Pour the sauce into a heat-safe vessel and cover the surface with plastic wrap to prevent a skin from forming. Allow the sauce to cool to room temperature before refrigerating.

Mushroom Sauté

Preheat a medium non-stick pan for a minute over medium-high heat. Add the mushrooms to the dry pan and gently begin stirring occasionally until the excess moisture from the mushrooms cooks off.

continued on next page

Once the mushrooms have released most of their moisture,
they should have browned slightly and smell a bit nutty. Add
1 Tbsp of the butter. Stirring occasionally, allow the mushrooms
to caramelize, about 2 minutes. Add the garlic and stir for
15 seconds–do not burn the garlic. Deglaze the pan by adding
the wine and stirring.

Add the parsley and the remaining 1 Tbsp butter and continue
to cook until the liquid has reduced by half. Remove from
the heat, season to taste with salt, and set aside until ready
to assemble the dish.

Assembly

Preheat the oven to 425°F.

In an oven-safe vessel, add the cooled Mornay sauce. (You
want to use a vessel that will allow the depth of the sauce to
be about 1 inch. Hearth uses cast-iron pans, but any small or
medium casserole dish should work just fine.) Place on a
baking sheet and bake until the sauce begins to bubble around
the edges.

Artfully spoon the mushroom mixture on top and serve
immediately to your adoring fans–preferably with a generous
side of toasted bread.

NOTE: *Some mushrooms will release lots of liquid, some not
so much. The goal is to remove most of the excess, thereby
intensifying the flavour.*

SPINACH DUMPLINGS

SERVES 4

DC: When the ground has finally thawed and spinach starts creeping up, you know the warmer weather is here to stay. One of Western Canada's top chefs—and Prairie Grid Dinner alumnus—Garrett Martin takes the tender spring greens and uses them in a simple yet stunning dumpling dish that will remind you that spring isn't so bad after all.

"Tasty, soft, and luxurious, these dumplings combine a dead-simple Italian preparation for gnudi with a Prairie spin on the French sauce amandine that is typically reserved for fish. If you like acidity, don't be shy about the vinegar and mustard for this dish—they help everything hang in balance with the rich brown butter and ricotta." —Garrett Martin, executive chef at Major Tom

Spinach Dumplings

- 1 lb ricotta
- 8 oz baby spinach
- ½ egg, beaten
- ½ cup all-purpose flour, plus more for dusting
- 1 tsp kosher salt, plus more for boiling dumplings

Almond and Brown Butter Sauce

- 3 Tbsp unsalted butter
- 2 Tbsp grainy Dijon mustard
- ¼ cup toasted slivered almonds
- 2 Tbsp finely chopped fresh flat-leaf parsley
- 1 Tbsp apple cider vinegar
- Kosher salt

Spinach Dumplings

Allow the ricotta to hang in a cheesecloth in a strainer or fine-mesh sieve set atop a large bowl in the fridge for at least 8 hours or overnight to drain excess whey.

Bring a medium pot of generously salted water to a rapid boil with a lid on. Add the spinach and replace the lid. Let the water return to a boil and cook the spinach until it is completely wilted and bright green but not mushy, approximately 20 seconds.

Strain the spinach and run it under cold water for 30 seconds to cool it down. Wrap the cooked and cooled spinach in a clean dish towel and squeeze as much water out of it as possible. (The more water you can wring out, the lighter your dumplings will be.) Coarsely chop the drained spinach.

Place the spinach, ricotta, egg, flour, and salt in a large mixing bowl. Stir gently with a spoon until the mixture is homogeneous. Do not overmix.

continued on next page

Dust a baking sheet with flour. Spoon little dumplings, about 1 inch in diameter, onto the prepared baking sheet. Roll the dumplings into nice spheres and roll them in the flour to cover completely. Let them sit while you prepare the sauce.

Almond and Brown Butter Sauce

Heat the butter in a small pot over medium heat until it browns and smells nutty, 6–7 minutes. Add the mustard and continue to cook for 1 minute.

Add the almonds, parsley, and vinegar. Stir to combine, then remove from the heat. Once cooled slightly, taste and season with salt as desired.

Bring a large pot of salted water to a simmer.

Shake the flour off the dumplings and, working in several batches, carefully drop them into the simmering water. Give them a light stir with a slotted spoon to keep them from sticking to each other or to the bottom of the pot. Cook for 45–60 seconds, until they begin to float.

Using a slotted spoon, carefully remove the dumplings and place them on a serving platter or plates. Generously pour the sauce over top and serve immediately.

MODERN BORSCHT

SERVES 4-6

DC: Borscht doesn't necessarily *need* a makeover, but it's getting one anyway! Though I am not of Ukrainian descent—rather, a hodgepodge of Acadian, Métis, German, and Scottish—borscht is a soup that is synonymous with Prairie cooking. It also is a dish that is widely enjoyed in the late fall and winter, but since snowstorms can be as common in April as in November, I say spring is a good time for this tasty soup. My version incorporates all of the elements you'll find in a traditional preparation, just presented in a different manner, more or less. The roasted cabbage adds extra umami to the stunningly pink soup, and transforming dill into a quick oil really makes everything pop when it comes to serving. This is definitely not your baba's borscht.

Borscht

1 Tbsp canola oil

1 yellow onion, diced

3 cloves garlic, chopped

1 cup diced carrots

1 cup diced celery

3 cups diced peeled russet potatoes

2 cups coarsely chopped pickled beets (try using Spicy Pickled Beets on page 84)

4 cups vegetable or beef broth

2 cups water

1 cup pickled beet juice

1 tsp dried dill

Salt

Roasted Red Cabbage

¼ small red cabbage, cut into ½-inch-thick slices

Canola oil, for drizzling

Salt

Borscht

Heat the oil in a large pot over medium-high heat. Add the onion, garlic, carrots, and celery and cook for 5 minutes, stirring occasionally. Add the potatoes and continue to cook for 5 minutes, stirring occasionally. The potatoes will soften slightly. Add the beets, broth, water, beet juice, and dried dill and bring the soup to a simmer. Reduce the heat to medium, cover, and cook for 15 minutes or until all the vegetables are fork-tender.

Use an immersion blender to purée the soup until smooth. Season to taste with salt and cook for 15 minutes more on low heat to allow the flavours to mingle. The soup can stay warm on the stove while you roast the cabbage.

Roasted Red Cabbage

Preheat the oven to 450°F.

Lay the cabbage pieces in an even layer on a baking sheet, drizzle with the oil, and season with the salt. Roast until the cabbage is tender and notably browned on top with crispy edges, about 18–20 minutes. Let cool slightly before serving with the soup.

Dill Oil

¼ cup coarsely chopped fresh dill

¼ cup cold-pressed canola oil

Splash pickle brine (or apple cider vinegar)

Assembly

¼ cup sour cream

2 Tbsp homogenized milk

Dill Oil

Combine the dill, oil, and pickle brine in a blender and purée to emulsify. Transfer to a bowl until ready to serve.

Assembly

Ladle the soup into bowls. Combine the sour cream and milk in a small bowl and use a spoon to drizzle it over top of the soup. Drizzle the dill oil over top as well, and garnish with the roasted cabbage. The soup can be frozen or kept in the fridge for up to 1 week in sealed containers. Store the soup components (soup, cabbage, dill oil, and cream mixture) separately.

IRISH BEEF STEW

SERVES 4

TC: Use up the last of your frozen and cellared vegetables to make this hearty beef stew. Guinness beer adds depth, and Dexter beef, an Irish breed known for its significant amount of marbling, makes for a luscious texture. In Edmonton, we're lucky to source Dexter beef from the Butchery by Rge Rd. Check the Canadian Dexter Cattle Association to find where Dexter cows are raised near you and then call a local butcher for availability.

1 cup all-purpose flour

2 tsp salt, plus more for seasoning

1 Tbsp black pepper

1½ lb Dexter stewing beef, cut into 2½-inch cubes

3 Tbsp canola oil, plus more as needed

1 large onion (yellow or white), peeled and chopped

4 cloves garlic, minced

1¼ cups Guinness beer (from a 330 mL can)

3½ cups beef broth

2 celery stalks, coarsely chopped

4 carrots, peeled and coarsely chopped

2 parsnips, peeled and coarsely chopped

1½ cups frozen peas

1½ cups waxy potatoes (red or white), coarsely chopped

3 Tbsp tomato paste

1 bay leaf

1 tsp dried thyme

In a large bowl, mix the flour with the salt and pepper. Add the beef and toss to coat.

Heat the oil in a large (9-quart) Dutch oven over medium heat. Brown the beef in three batches, on all sides, for about 40 seconds per side. Set aside the browned beef in a deep dish to catch the juices. Do not throw out the seasoned flour; you'll need it in a few more steps.

Add the onion to the pot. You might have to add a bit more oil if it has gone too dry. Sauté for 3–5 minutes, add the garlic, and let it sweat for a few minutes. Add the reserved seasoned flour and stir to coat the onions.

Gradually add the beer while stirring and scraping up the browned bits with a wooden spoon.

Add the browned beef with its juices, plus the broth, celery, carrots, parsnips, peas, potatoes, tomato paste, bay leaf, and thyme. Bring to a boil, and then turn the heat to low, cover, and simmer for 90 minutes. Before serving, taste the sauce. Season with more salt, if needed.

NOTE: *If you can't source Dexter beef, look for regular stewing beef that has a good amount of connective tissue.*

BARLEY AND HEMP HEART RISOTTO WITH BRESAOLA AND PROSCIUTTO CRISPS

SERVES 4–5

DC: When it comes to dishes that scale easily, risotto is ideal. As long as you've got the pots and pans, it's just as easy to make for four people as it is for twelve.

Here, we're skipping the usual arborio rice and celebrating two different Prairie-grown ingredients instead: barley and hemp hearts. One thing I really love about barley, especially in the risotto process, is that it is pretty forgiving of overcooking. Even the best cooks make mistakes in the kitchen, so bless barley for being able to cover for them on occasion. The baked-off bresaola and prosciutto garnish adds a lovely crunch to this otherwise creamy, indulgent dish.

Bresaola and Prosciutto Crisps

8 thin slices of bresaola

4 thin slices of prosciutto

Barley and Hemp Heart Risotto

5 cups chicken broth

1 Tbsp cold-pressed canola oil

1 yellow onion, diced

2–3 Tbsp water

2 Tbsp butter

1 clove garlic, minced

1½ cups pot barley, rinsed well

½ cup hemp hearts

1 cup half and half cream

2 cups mixed greens (like mustard greens, chicory, spinach, arugula)

½ cup grated butter cheese (I use Lakeside Farmstead Alberta Butter Cheese)

Salt

Bresaola and Prosciutto Crisps

Preheat the oven to 400°F. Line a baking sheet with parchment paper.

Place the bresaola and prosciutto slices on the prepared baking sheet and cook until crispy, 12–14 minutes. Remove from the oven and let cool.

Barley and Hemp Heart Risotto

Bring the broth to a near-simmer in a medium pot. Reduce to low heat and keep hot.

Heat the oil over medium-high heat in a large deep pan. Add the onion and cook for 5 minutes or until it starts to brown lightly. Add 2 Tbsp of the water to the pan and continue to cook for 5 minutes, stirring occasionally. The onions should deepen in colour noticeably, but add more water to slow browning as needed. We are aiming for a golden colour here.

continued on next page

Add the butter and garlic to the pan. Cook until the garlic is fragrant, about 2 minutes, and then add the barley. Stir well and allow the barley to absorb the butter. Once there is hardly any visible liquid in the pan, add about 1 cup of the hot broth. Stir frequently until absorbed. Continue this process four more times until approximately 1 cup of broth remains. This should take 18–20 minutes in total. Add the hemp hearts to the pan and stir to incorporate.

Add the cream to the pot with the remaining broth and allow it to heat up before continuing to ladle the mixture into the pan of risotto. Once the last bit of broth mixture has been added to the pan, stir in the greens and cheese. Continue to cook and stir until the greens have wilted and the cheese has melted. The risotto should thicken slightly. An al dente texture is the goal here, so have a taste of the barley risotto to check to see if you're on the mark. You can season with salt as desired at this point, and cook slightly longer if needed.

To serve, portion among plates or bowls and top with the bresaola and prosciutto crisps.

ROASTED FARMER SAUSAGE WITH SPINACH AND MUSTARD CREAM SAUCE

SERVES 3–4

DC: Some like to say "farmer's," others say "farmer." Regardless of how you may choose to address it, this type of sausage is a tried-and-true fridge staple in households across the Prairies. Growing up, we'd often eat this sausage cold, sliced up with some cheddar slices and soda crackers as a quick snack, but it wasn't until I was an adult that I truly appreciated it at its best: when roasted or grilled. I love roasting farmer sausage in a cast-iron frying pan and then using its residual juices to flavour vegetables like the spinach in this recipe. This dish is uncomplicated and very rewarding. When it comes to the sauce, mustard can often be more punchy than simply "tangy," so a little bit of sour cream really helps smooth things out here.

Roasted Farmer Sausage

18 oz farmer sausage link, cut into 4 equal portions

1 Tbsp canola oil

Mustard Cream Sauce

2 Tbsp canola oil, divided

1 yellow onion, diced

2 cloves garlic, minced

2 Tbsp water

1 Tbsp butter

1 Tbsp all-purpose flour, plus more as needed

1 cup half and half cream

1 Tbsp grainy Dijon mustard

1 Tbsp Dijon mustard

2 Tbsp sour cream

Salt

Roasted Farmer Sausage

Preheat the oven to 400°F.

On the diagonal, score the top of the sausage pieces, then place in a shallow baking dish or heat-safe pan. Drizzle with the canola oil and toss to evenly coat. Roast until the tops begin to split and the casing becomes crispy, about 25 minutes.

Mustard Cream Sauce

While the sausage is roasting, heat 1 Tbsp of the canola oil in a small pot over medium-high heat. Once hot, add the onion and garlic and cook for 5 minutes, stirring frequently.

Add the water and butter. Once the butter has melted, stir the onion mixture and then lightly sprinkle the flour evenly across its surface. Continue to stir for 10–15 seconds. The onion mixture should have a paste-like texture. Add a touch more flour if this is not the case.

continued on next page

Wilted Spinach

3 Tbsp water

1 Tbsp honey

1 Tbsp honey vinegar (or apple cider vinegar)

1 pinch salt, plus more tor seasoning

1 bunch spinach, washed and ends trimmed

Add the cream and continue to stir for 1 minute. You should now have a sauce that is thick enough to coat the back of a spoon, but not too viscous. Reduce the heat to low and stir in the grainy mustard, Dijon mustard, and sour cream. Taste and add salt to taste. Keep warm on the stove until ready to serve.

Wilted Spinach

In a medium pan, heat the water, honey, vinegar, and salt together over medium heat. Once the honey has dissolved, add the spinach and cook until the spinach is fully wilted, 2–3 minutes. Season with salt to taste.

Assembly

Remove the sausage from its baking dish and set on a plate. Add the wilted spinach to the baking dish and, using tongs, toss gently to coat the greens with the pan juices. Nestle the sausage back into the dish with the spinach and serve with the warm mustard cream sauce on the side.

VEGETARIAN TOURTIÈRE WITH RHUBARB AND SASKATOON RELISH

SERVES 6–8

DC: This vegetarian spin on the classic tourtière from Edmonton chef Steve Brochu of MilkCrate is perfect for one of those unexpectedly snowy days in the springtime. Locally cultivated mushrooms and herbs are still widely available, and you can use up those last few russet potatoes that are taking up space at your favourite farmers' market stall. The rhubarb and Saskatoon relish is absolutely delicious and can also be used on everything from charcuterie boards to sandwiches, burgers, and more.

"Traditionally, tourtière is served with fruit ketchup, which is very tasty too, but this easy relish is a great example of how Alberta-grown ingredients can come together to make a great condiment." —Steve Brochu, owner of Edmonton's MilkCrate

Pie Crust

2¼ cups all-purpose flour

¼ tsp salt

1 Tbsp granulated sugar

⅔ cup butter, cold and cubed

1 large egg

1 Tbsp water

Tourtière Filling

3 Tbsp canola oil

4 portobello mushrooms, shredded with a grater

Salt and pepper

1 yellow onion, diced

4 cloves garlic, minced

6 button mushrooms, sliced

½ tsp cinnamon

¼ tsp ground cloves

Pie Crust

Place the flour, salt, sugar, butter, egg, and water in a food processor and blitz until crumbly. Turn out onto plastic wrap and force the dough together with your hands. Wrap tightly with the plastic wrap and let rest for at least 2 hours in the fridge before using.

Tourtière Filling

Heat the oil in a large pot or deep frying pan over medium heat. Once hot, sauté the grated portobello mushroom until it starts to brown slightly. Transfer to a paper towel–lined plate and season with a touch of salt and pepper.

In the same pot you cooked the mushrooms in, add the onion and garlic and cook until golden, stirring occasionally, about 12 minutes. Add the button mushrooms and continue to cook over medium heat until the mushrooms have reduced in size by half.

Reduce the heat to low. Add the cinnamon, cloves, allspice, thyme, and rosemary, and return the portobello mushrooms

continued on next page

½ tsp allspice

2 sprigs fresh thyme, leaves
    removed

1 sprig fresh rosemary, leaves
    removed and finely chopped

1 large unpeeled russet potato,
    grated

1 tsp honey

⅓ cup dry white wine

1 cup vegetable broth

Rhubarb and Saskatoon Relish

2 cups fresh or frozen sliced
    rhubarb

2 cups diced yellow onion

½ cup apple cider vinegar

¾ cup packed brown sugar

1 Tbsp salt

1 tsp cinnamon

1 tsp ground ginger

1 tsp allspice

½ tsp black pepper

1 cup fresh or frozen Saskatoon
    berries

Assembly

1 egg + 1 Tbsp water, whisked, for
    the egg wash

to the pot and cook for 30 minutes, stirring occasionally, to allow the flavours to intensify.

Add the potato, honey, wine, and vegetable broth. Increase the heat to medium and bring to a simmer. Simmer until the potatoes are cooked through and the mixture has thickened, about 15 minutes. Season to taste with salt, remove from the heat, and allow to cool until you are ready to assemble the tourtières.

Rhubarb and Saskatoon Relish

Combine the rhubarb, onion, vinegar, sugar, salt, cinnamon, ginger, allspice, pepper, and berries in a medium pot and bring to a simmer over medium high heat. Stirring occasionally, cook until the onion and rhubarb soften and break down, 25–30 minutes. Let cool for 10 minutes, then blitz to a coarse texture in a food processor or blender. Transfer to a sealed container and store in the fridge until ready to serve. This relish will keep in the fridge for up to 1 week.

Assembly

Preheat the oven to 350°F. Grease a 9-inch pie pan.

Split the dough into two equal parts and roll out each to a thickness of 1/6 inch.

Place the first portion of dough over the prepared pie pan and press in gently to form. Trim the excess dough around the edges. Add the filling to the pie pan and fill to the brim. Press down gently with your hands to help compact the filling slightly. Place the remaining portion of rolled-out dough on top. Crinkle the edges and cut four or five small slits with a knife to allow steam to vent.

Brush liberally with the egg wash and bake until the pastry is cooked through and the top is golden brown, about 25 minutes. Allow to cool slightly before slicing and serving with the relish on the side.

SOUR CREAM PANNA COTTA WITH STEWED FRUIT

SERVES 6

DC: If you're like me and you don't excel at making desserts (no shame in that), a panna cotta can be a person's best friend. Positive attributes of a panna cotta can include, but are not limited to: easy to make in advance, a blank canvas to add your favourite flavours to, and quite lovely words to say out loud. Jokes aside, my take on panna cotta incorporates sour cream for a bit of tang, which gives it a can't-quite-put-your-finger-on-it flavour that your friends will love. For the topping, dried Saskatoon berries come alive wonderfully when rehydrated in a mixture of currant wine, brown sugar, and butter. Add some locally grown pear if you can get your hands on any remaining cellared stock—otherwise feel free to leave it out.

Sour Cream Panna Cotta

2 tsp gelatin

1 cup homogenized milk

2 cups heavy (35%) cream

½ cup sour cream

½ tsp vanilla paste or pure vanilla extract

⅓ cup granulated sugar

Stewed Fruit

½ cup dried Saskatoon berries (or dried cranberries or dried blueberries)

¼ cup Living Sky Winery currant wine (or similar fruit wine)

2 Tbsp brown sugar

2 Tbsp butter

1 cup diced Bartlett pears

Sour Cream Panna Cotta

Place the gelatin and milk in a small bowl and whisk to combine. Set aside.

Place the cream, sour cream, vanilla, and sugar in a medium pot and bring to a near-simmer over medium-high heat (you're looking for the liquid to be steaming, but not bubbling). Add the milk and gelatin mixture to the pot and whisk until completely dissolved, 2–3 minutes.

Spray the interior of six small 6 oz ramekins with cooking spray or dab a paper towel in some canola oil and rub the interiors to coat them.

Evenly ladle the hot liquid into the ramekins, leaving about ½ inch of space from the lip. Refrigerate and let the panna cottas set, about 4 hours.

Stewed Fruit

Place the berries, wine, brown sugar, and butter in a small pot and bring to a simmer over medium-high heat. Reduce to low heat and cook until the berries soften considerably and the

continued on next page

liquid reduces by half, about 5 minutes. Add the pears and cook for several minutes more. Cool to room temperature before serving.

Assembly

Take the panna cottas out of the fridge 15 minutes before serving to allow them to warm up slightly (this will result in a smoother, creamier texture). Place a generous spoonful of stewed fruit over top of each and serve.

NOTE: *Both the panna cottas and stewed fruit can be made several days in advance. The stewed fruit goes perfectly with pancakes too. Just saying . . .*

RHUBARB GALETTE

SERVES 8

TC: While technically a vegetable, rhubarb presents as a fruit and easily works in recipes for baked goods or compotes. Depending on the variety, a rhubarb stalk can be green, pink, or bright red. It's the season's early riser, usually poking its leafy head through the soil in April and becoming ready to eat in June. If you don't have your own plant and can't acquire some stalks by way of alley raids, you can find rhubarb at farmers' markets throughout the summer. A galette is like an open-faced pie, and it's the perfect recipe for beginner cooks because it's easy to assemble and looks refined when baked, even with its semi-rustic appearance.

2½ cups chopped rhubarb stalks

1 Tbsp cornstarch

⅓ cup granulated sugar

1 tsp vanilla

2 store-bought 10 × 10-inch frozen butter puff pastry sheets (16 oz)

2 Tbsp whole milk

1 Tbsp coarse raw sugar, for topping (optional)

Add the rhubarb, cornstarch, sugar, and vanilla to a medium bowl and toss to combine.

Place the pastry sheets on a floured surface and cut each sheet into 4 equal squares (you'll have 8 squares total). Once the squares have been cut, place them on to two parchment-lined baking sheets.

Divide the rhubarb mixture equally between the 8 portions of dough and fold the edges up, pinching together the folds as you work your way around the square. Leave the centre open to expose the fruit.

Preheat the oven to 350°F.

Brush the pastry edges with the milk and set the galettes in the fridge to chill for 30 minutes. This helps the galettes keep their shape while baking.

Remove the galettes from the fridge. Sprinkle the tops with coarse sugar, and bake for 25–30 minutes, until the pastry is golden brown and the filling is bubbling.

Let cool on a cooling rack. When the galettes are completely cooled, they can be stored in a lidded container on the counter for up to 2 days.

MERINGUE NESTS WITH WILD BLUEBERRY COMPOTE

SERVES 8

TC: Meringue nests are easy to make and fun to eat. The preparation only takes about 10 minutes, but baking them will require several hours, so keep that in mind when planning your day. These airy receptacles will hold any fresh or preserved fruit. We're using the Fruit Compote (page 265) made of frozen wild blueberries from last year's harvest to help bridge the fruit gap until the summer crops are ready. And remember, compotes aren't just for dessert; they add pizzazz to charcuterie boards and make wonderful complements to dishes like roast pork or turkey.

Meringues

4 egg whites, at room temperature

¾ cup superfine sugar

¼ tsp pure vanilla extract

½ tsp cream of tartar

Assembly

1 cup Fruit Compote (page 265) made with blueberries

Fresh basil or mint, for garnish

NOTE: *Baked meringues require egg whites only, which means you'll have some egg yolks hanging around. We suggest using them for Aioli (page 261) or to make the custard in our Haskap Flapper Pie Cups (page 55).*

Meringues

Preheat the oven to 250°F and place racks at the middle and lower levels. Line two baking sheets with parchment paper.

Place the egg whites in a large, dry bowl and beat at medium speed until foamy. Increase the speed and beat until thick and opaque. Slowly add the sugar and beat until stiff peaks form. The whole process should take about 8 minutes.

If you have a piping bag, this is the time to use it: attach a ½-inch-diameter star nozzle to the bag and fill the bag with meringue. Pipe the meringue onto the parchment paper by starting with a ½-inch dot and then making concentric circles until your base is about 3 inches across. Pipe one more layer on top of that base, leaving the middle unfilled, so that the exterior wall of the nest is 1 inch high.

If you don't have a piping bag, a large spoon will also work. Just scoop out the meringue and plop it on the prepared baking sheet. Use the bottom of the spoon to make an indent to hold the fruit.

Bake for 3 hours or until crisp and dry. Test for doneness by tapping lightly with a fork. If the meringues feel spongy, turn off the oven and let them sit for another hour. Store in a sealed container at room temperature for up to 2 weeks, or freeze in layers between parchment paper in a sealed container for up to 3 months.

Assembly

To assemble the dessert, plate the meringues and place about 2 Tbsp of the compote in the indent of each meringue. Garnish with fresh mint or basil, and dig in. Half the fun is breaking the meringues, the other half is eating them!

THE CAESAR

SERVES 1

TC: In 1969, Walter Chell, a food and beverage worker at the Calgary Inn, invented a vodka and tomato juice cocktail and called it the Caesar. While it was a smash hit on the Prairies, and eventually accepted nationwide, it is still a drink you don't often find on a menu outside Canada. Like all classic cocktails, Caesar riffs have sprouted up over the years. For instance, a Caesar made with gin is called a Beefeater. A Caesar made with white rum is a Clamdigger, and a Caesar with whisky, a Stampeder. Whatever your poison, find a tomato-clam cocktail mix you like, add your spirit of choice, garnish with anything you can think of, and bottoms up.

While it is said that Mr. Chell added salt and oregano but no Tabasco, we're going with a slightly different version, as Worcestershire sauce and most clam-cocktail mixes already contain salt, and we think Tabasco is a great all-around hot sauce found in most peoples' pantries. What you use as a garnish is only limited by what you have in your fridge or pantry: pickled vegetables, a celery stalk, a stick of jerky, crispy bacon, a skewer laced with jumbo shrimp or tiny tomatoes with bocconcini . . . go with what you've got; truly, the wide-open Prairie sky is the limit.

2 tsp + 1 shake celery salt, divided

1 lime wedge

1½ oz vodka

2 dashes Tabasco hot sauce

4 dashes Worcestershire sauce

3 grinds freshly cracked black pepper

1 tsp lime juice (about a wedge's worth)

4 oz Caesar cocktail mix (see note)

Celery stalk, for garnish

Place 2 tsp of the celery salt in a shallow dish. Circle the rim of a tall glass with the lime wedge, then dip the rim into the celery salt.

Add the vodka, hot sauce, Worcestershire sauce, pepper, the remaining 1 shake of celery salt, and a squirt of fresh lime juice (plus the spent lime wedge) to the glass, fill it with ice, add the cocktail mix, and stir. Garnish with the celery stalk.

N O T E : *Mott's Clamato Caesar cocktail mix still holds an iron grip on the choice of mix to use, but the world of clam-tomato drink mixes has been blown wide open, so go forth and taste: find one you like and go with it. No one's going to judge.*

NORTHERN JULEP

SERVES 1

TC: From low-alcohol session meads to crisp, herbal 10-percenters, the refreshing meads of today are turning heads from coast to coast and converting skeptics along the way. Many of these modern meads are best served over ice, but they also work well in cocktails. We partnered Sawyer, a lightly hopped, carbonated mead from Tamarack Jack's with Peat & Smoke, a Canadian single malt whisky whose subtle smokiness complements the herbal flavours of this enticing Alberta drink. Some mint, crushed ice, and a wee bit of simple syrup are used to make a northern version of the Mint Julep, the official cocktail of the Kentucky Derby held every May in Louisville. Cheers, y'all . . . or perhaps, "Cheers, eh?" would be more appropriate.

4–6 fresh mint leaves

¾ oz Basic Simple Syrup (page 273)

3 oz dry mead

Crushed ice

1 oz whisky

Fresh mint, for garnish

Put the mint and simple syrup in a julep cup or rocks glass and gently muddle.

Add the mead and fill the cup halfway with crushed ice. Stir with a bar spoon. Add the whisky and top with enough crushed ice to make it almost like a snow cone. The idea is to have the ice slowly melt and dilute the whisky as you sip. Garnish with fresh mint and drink with a straw.

STAPLES

STAPLES IN YOUR PANTRY, FRIDGE,

or freezer are items that can stand alone but turn into something completely different and wonderful with a few tweaks. Any vegetable can be eaten raw or cooked, but add the peels (especially from carrots, celery, and onions) to some wilting herbs and water, let it simmer, and you've got broth, which, in turn, can be made into soup, gravy, or a finishing sauce for a juicy steak.

A couple of eggs made into an omelette can easily serve as breakfast or lunch, but whisk oil into egg yolks and you've got a condiment that's perfect for slathering on bread for a sandwich. Add minced garlic and presto, and you've now made aioli.

Have some pieces of bread that are a little less than fresh, or crusts that got left behind? Tear old bread into cubes, put them on top of soup, add some shredded cheese, and broil. Or cut the bread into chunks, throw them in a pan, drizzle them with oil, and brown under the broiler to make croutons that will taste better than anything packaged in a box from a store.

And if your fridge is overstocked with milk, cream, or yogurt, all you need to do is add an acid like apple cider vinegar, and you've got ricotta to spread on crostini or use in a pasta dish. Too many berries and not enough people to eat them? Rinse them, towel dry them, place them on a baking sheet in the freezer, and transfer them to a container once they've frozen. When you need to make a syrup or sauce, there they are, ready to use. These tips and tricks are easy to learn and yield huge payoffs.

ROASTED SHALLOTS AND GARLIC

MAKES 1½ CUPS

TC: Make the most of the garlic and shallot harvest by turning them into an at-the-ready flavour bomb to use when roasting meats or vegetables, like a marinade of sorts. It's a required ingredient in the pear jam used in Pear and Brie Tarts with Roasted Shallots and Garlic on page 104. It's also great in salad dressings—we use it in the Roasted Shallot, Garlic, and Feta Dressing on page 268.

6 large shallots (about 10 oz), sliced into rounds

10 cloves garlic, peeled, smashed, and halved

1 cup canola oil

Preheat the oven to 300°F.

Combine the ingredients in a baking dish and cover with tinfoil. Set in the oven. Stir after 30 minutes. After 1 hour, stir again, take the foil off, and continue roasting for a final 30 minutes.

Let cool, pour into a sealable jar, and store in the fridge for up to 2 weeks.

MRKT FRESH RICOTTA

MAKES 2 CUPS

TC: Ricotta is a versatile soft cheese that is super easy to make at home. I've made wonderful ricotta from cream and milk of varying fat percentages, but Edmonton chef, Carla Alexander, uses sour cream and homogenized milk, which results in a soft, creamy ricotta that is next level. The recipe, as laid out below, is what she used at her former restaurant, MRKT. And don't toss the whey (the liquid that remains after the cheese is formed)! It can be used in marinades or braising applications as we do with the leeks on page 78.

8 cups homogenized milk

1 cup full-fat sour cream or Balkan yogurt

1 tsp sea salt

2 tsp vinegar (see note)

Whisk the milk and sour cream together in a pot. Add the salt and heat over medium heat until the milk reaches the simmering point. If you have an instant-read thermometer, the milk should be at about 185°F. Add the vinegar and turn the heat off. Do not stir.

Lay a cheesecloth in a medium sieve and set over a bowl of about the same size. Using a ladle, scoop the mixture from the pot into the cheesecloth and let the curds drain for 5–15 minutes. The longer it drains, the drier your curds will be.

Enjoy the curds immediately or store in a lidded container in the fridge and use within 1 week. The whey can be kept for up to 1 week in a lidded container in the fridge as well, or in the freezer for up to 2 months.

NOTE: *Most vinegars will work, even the ones flavoured with herbs. I avoid dark vinegars like balsamic or black, though, because their flavours are too prominent and the end result will be an unappealing shade of grey. Lemon juice works very well and is great for ricotta that is used in a dessert.*

SEA BUCKTHORN JUICE

MAKES 1 CUP

TC: The sea buckthorn is a deciduous bush native to Europe and Asia and introduced into Canada in the 1800s. If left untended, the plant is known to quickly spread and is considered invasive. However, the berries of the bush have long been known for their nutritional content and used in pharmaceutical and cosmetic applications, so the berry itself is quite treasured.

The bush is drought and salt resistant and grows just as well along highways as it does now planted in orchards. The berries are about the size of cranberries and are highly acidic. The flavour of the berry's juice is similar to lemon and works well as a substitute in recipes where lemon juice is required, like in our Alberta Sour (page 133) or in the aioli that accompanies the Bacon-Wrapped Asparagus (page 200). If you can't find fresh berries in orchards or in the wild, check your local grocery store's freezer section.

2 cups fresh or frozen sea buckthorn berries

1 cup water

To a small pot, add the berries and water and bring to a boil. Turn the heat down and simmer for 10 minutes.

Place a medium fine-mesh sieve over a bowl and add the softened berries. Press gently with the back of a large spoon or cocktail muddler to extract as much juice as you can from the berries. The pulp that remains can be discarded.

Store the juice in a jar in the fridge for up to 1 month. Shake before use.

AIOLI

MAKES 1½ CUPS

TC: The word "aioli" is a combination of two French words: garlic (ail) and oil (olio). To make a traditional aioli, garlic and salt are combined to make a paste, and oil is added and whisked to the point of emulsification. Quite often, an egg yolk is added to enhance the emulsification process, as we have done here.

The wonderful part about making your own aioli is that you can add a variety of seasonings or other ingredients to alter the flavour but still keep the base intact. Check your cupboard and fridge. If you've got capers or hot sauce or mustard or herbs, a whole new world of condiments has just been placed at your feet—or, in this case, on your table.

Grab some local garlic, a couple of egg yolks, and some canola oil and get whiskin'. Our aioli is the perfect accompaniment to grilled steak, steamed new potatoes, or fish.

4 cloves garlic, minced

½ tsp kosher salt, plus more for seasoning

2 egg yolks

1½ Tbsp apple cider vinegar

1 cup canola oil

½ tsp white pepper

Add the garlic and salt to a mortar and use a pestle to grind into a paste.

To a large bowl, add the egg yolks and vinegar and whisk until blended. Add the garlic paste and blend. Slowly whisk in the oil until the mixture emulsifies and thickens into a sauce. Add the pepper and whisk to incorporate.

Taste the aioli and season with a bit more salt (if needed). Store in a lidded container in the fridge, and mark the date on the label. Because this recipe contains raw egg yolks, it should be consumed within 4 days.

SEA BUCKTHORN AIOLI

To make sea buckthorn aioli, replace the apple cider vinegar with an equal amount of Sea Buckthorn Juice (page 260).

CROUTONS

MAKES 4 CUPS

TC: Dan and I have different crouton styles: I like mine uniform and made from dense bread like sourdough; he likes his croutons hand-torn and made of an airy bread like a French loaf. This is on par for our personalities, now that I think about it: if we were dancers, Dan's specialty would be interpretive, mine would be the two-step . . . or the polka, if I really let loose. In the realm of croutons, neither style is better than the other, but each is better suited to particular recipes. The croutons used in the Leeks a' Whey au Gratin (page 82) are smaller to fit the bowl and made from sourdough so that they cradle the cheese but don't sink because they're saturated with broth. The croutons used in the Brassica (Sort of) Caesar Salad (page 88) are made from a French loaf so that they provide textural relief while acting as delectable morsels on their own when coated in salad dressing. Either way, store-bought croutons can't hold a candle to any style of homemade croutons in flavour, texture, price, or looks. Below is a recipe for croutons you'd use in a soup or salad—the type that look store-bought, but taste way better.

½ loaf sourdough or potato bread, coarsely cut into 1 × 1-inch pieces

½ cup canola oil

2 tsp garlic powder (optional)

1 tsp sea salt

Line a baking sheet with parchment paper.

Place the bread cubes in a large bowl, drizzle with the oil, then sprinkle with the garlic powder and salt. Toss to coat and place on the prepared baking sheet.

Set the oven rack to the second position from the top and turn the broiler to high. Let the element heat up for a minute before placing the pan on the rack.

Check the croutons every 30 seconds to ensure the bread isn't burning. Turn the cubes over and broil until evenly browned. This should only take 2–3 minutes.

HAND-TORN GARLIC BREAD

MAKES 1 LOAF

DC: I have many fond memories from my youth of watching in anticipation as my mom or dad pulled a hot tinfoil-wrapped French loaf from the oven. My siblings and I knew that this loaf, sliced up, slathered with garlic butter, and reformed, would be hitting the table soon, and we were often more excited about grabbing our fair (and occasionally unfair) shares of garlic bread than we were about whatever the main course happened to be.

Nowadays, I like to take a slightly different approach to garlic bread, choosing to tear large pieces off the loaf and tossing the chunks in a garlic butter mixture before baking. This method offers more crispy bits on each piece of bread while still retaining a soft centre.

½ cup butter

1 clove garlic, smashed but intact

1 tsp garlic powder

1 tsp salt

1 tsp ground black pepper

1 French loaf, torn into 3-inch chunks

Maldon salt

Preheat the oven to 425°F.

Melt the butter in a small pot over low heat. Add the garlic, remove from the heat, and allow to infuse for 5 minutes. Discard the garlic and add the garlic powder, salt, and pepper to the butter. Stir to combine.

Working in two batches, place the bread chunks in a large mixing bowl, drizzle with some of the butter mixture, and toss until evenly coated.

Spread the bread on two baking sheets and toast in the oven until the edges start to brown but the bread is still soft in the centre, 10–12 minutes. Finish with Maldon salt if desired. Allow to cool slightly before serving.

NOTE: *You can make croutons with this recipe by tearing the bread into 1-inch pieces and baking for 18–20 minutes so the bread becomes crisp throughout.*

ROASTED VEGETABLE BROTH

MAKES 8 CUPS

TC: Vegetable broth is versatile and can be used in most recipes that call for broths. Roasting the vegetables deepens the flavour as well as the colour. Don't get stuck on the specific amounts here. If you have more carrots, use them. If you don't have leeks, that's okay. If you have all leeks and no onions, perfect. Just use up what you've collected over the past week or two, including onion skins, vegetable peels, tired parsnips, mushrooms, and wilted herbs. All of these ingredients can also be kept in the freezer—just find a large enough container that you can keep adding ingredients to and you'll never be caught short.

3 cloves garlic, skin on

2 leeks, split and washed, or 1 cup green parts or white ends

1 large onion, halved, skin on

3 unpeeled carrots or 1 cup carrot ends

3 celery stalks or 1 cup celery ends

3 parsnips or 1 cup parsnip peels or ends

1 cup fresh mushrooms, any kind will work

2 sprigs fresh thyme

1 handful fresh curly or flat-leaf parsley

1 bay leaf

3 Tbsp canola oil

2 tsp salt

10 cups water

Preheat the oven to 325°F.

Add the garlic, leeks, onion, carrots, celery, parsnips, mushrooms, thyme, parsley, and bay leaf to a large roaster, drizzle with the oil, and sprinkle with the salt.

Roast for 1 hour, stirring once or twice. Add the water to the roaster and let cook in the oven for another hour.

Remove from the oven, let cool, and strain out the cooked vegetables and herbs with a large slotted spoon. Pour the remaining contents through a cheesecloth or a sieve set over a large bowl.

Portion out into containers and freeze, or store in the fridge for up to 1 week.

FRUIT COMPOTE
MAKES 1½ CUPS

TC: Once you make one compote, you will view every seasonal fruit as a possible compote. This sweet condiment can top pancakes or ice cream, fill pastry cups, be incorporated into barbecue sauces, or cozy up next to roasted meats, just like the ubiquitous cranberry sauce that makes its appearance every Thanksgiving and Christmas. Regardless of what fruit you're planning to use, from field berries to rhubarb and stone fruit like peaches and pears, this is a baseline recipe that won't let you down.

2 cups fruit, fresh or frozen

¼ cup water

¼ cup granulated sugar (see note)

2 tsp fresh lemon juice

1 tsp vanilla

1 tsp cornstarch dissolved in 1 Tbsp water

Mix all of the ingredients in a small saucepan and bring to a boil. Turn the heat down and simmer for 10 minutes or until thickened. The compote should be saucy but still have noticeable chunks of fruit.

Store the compote in a lidded container in the fridge for up to 1 month.

NOTES: *1. If using rhubarb, add ½ cup of sugar for 2 cups of fruit. 2. Substituting maple syrup or honey for some or all of the sugar is fine, just know that the end product will have flavours of maple or whatever floral or herbaceous notes are prominent in the honey. If you want the flavour of the fruit to remain true, granulated white sugar is the best option. 3. If you've missed finding fruit that is fresh, all is not lost, as smaller, more locally minded grocers often have locally grown fruit that's frozen for out-of-season use.*

VINAIGRETTES AND DRESSINGS

Once you start making your own, you will never buy store-bought dressings again. You can get wildly creative or stick to an all-purpose dressing like the Apple Cider Vinaigrette (page 269). Here are a few of our favourite vinaigrette recipes that range from traditional to a little more unique using elixirs, pulp, and roasted items from some of our other dishes.

HERBED BUTTERMILK DRESSING
MAKES 1½ CUPS

TC: Once, on returning from Europe, Dan gifted me a bottle of herbed vinegar that he sampled in Prague. I loved it and treasured every drop of it. I can't find that specific brand in Alberta, but adding sugar and spices plus a blend of fresh herbs to white wine vinegar makes a close second. Use any combination of fresh herbs that appeal to you, but I find soft herbs like basil, dill, parsley, and tarragon work best.

½ cup buttermilk

1 Tbsp white wine vinegar

½ tsp granulated sugar

½ tsp celery salt

½ tsp garlic powder

1 Tbsp chopped fresh flat-leaf parsley

1 Tbsp chopped fresh basil

1 Tbsp chopped fresh tarragon

¼ tsp kosher salt

Freshly ground black pepper

¾ cup canola oil

Add the buttermilk, vinegar, sugar, celery salt, garlic powder, parsley, basil, tarragon, salt, and pepper to a pint-sized jar and stir with a fork until combined. Slowly add the oil while using an immersion blender to emulsify the ingredients. After about 1 minute, the mixture should be thick and creamy. Keep in a sealed container in the fridge and use within 2 weeks.

ROASTED SHALLOT, GARLIC, AND FETA DRESSING

MAKES 1½ CUPS

TC: If you've made the Roasted Shallots and Garlic on page 257, then this dressing is a good excuse to use some of its resulting flavoured oil. No need for salt as the feta contains enough on its own; season with crushed peppercorns and you're done. Add a half cup of this zippy mix to seasonal fresh vegetables or use as a dip for crudités any time of year.

½ cup oil from Roasted Shallots and Garlic (page 257)

3 Tbsp Alchemist Vinegar Honey Lemon Vinegar (see note)

1½ cups feta (about 9 oz)

1 tsp crushed pink peppercorns

Add all ingredients to a blender or mini food processor and blend until the dressing is thick and no large chunks of feta remain. Store the dressing in a lidded container in the fridge and use within 1 week.

NOTE: *If you can't source Alchemist vinegar, substitute a blend of 2½ Tbsp white wine vinegar, 1 tsp honey, and 1 tsp lemon juice.*

STRAWBERRY VINAIGRETTE

MAKES ¾ CUP

TC: Make the Spiced Strawberries (page 61) and you not only have that delicious dish to enjoy but the leftover elixir can be used to form the base of this summer berry vinaigrette which is light in body but packed with flavour. It's as delicious over delicate butter leaf lettuce as it is over a mixture of robust arugula and spinach.

1 Tbsp minced shallot

1 clove garlic, lightly crushed

1 Tbsp apple cider vinegar

¼ tsp salt

3 grinds of fresh black pepper

¼ cup elixir from Spiced Strawberries (page 61)

⅓ cup canola oil

To a small bowl, add the shallot, garlic, vinegar, salt, and pepper. Let the mixture sit for 5 minutes to allow the flavours to meld. Remove the garlic and discard. Stir in the elixir.

Add the oil while whisking to emulsify the ingredients. Alternatively, use a lidded glass jar instead of a bowl and shake it after adding the oil. Taste, adjust the seasoning, and remove the garlic. Store the vinaigrette in a lidded container in the fridge and use within 1 week.

ROASTED TOMATO VINAIGRETTE

MAKES ½ CUP

TC: If you're down to the last bits of the Stovetop Tomato Confit (page 22), then that pulpy oil at the bottom is perfectly seasoned oil for this vinaigrette. All you need to add is a vinegar (balsamic, in this case) and a bit of sweetener to dress some tender leafy greens like butter lettuce.

⅓ cup oil with pulp from Stovetop Tomato Confit (page 22)

2 Tbsp balsamic vinegar

3 tsp honey

1 tsp grainy mustard

¼ tsp salt

3 grinds of fresh black pepper

Add the tomato confit oil, vinegar, honey, mustard, salt, and pepper to a small jar and shake until emulsified. Taste and add more salt and pepper if needed. Store the vinaigrette in a lidded container in the fridge and use within 1 week.

APPLE CIDER VINAIGRETTE

MAKES ½ CUP

TC: This versatile dressing can be used for almost any salad you can dream up. It's easy to make and nicely balanced without any one ingredient hogging the spotlight. You can buy this basic dressing from the store, but it'll come with a load of preservatives, colour enhancers, and things to keep it shelf stable, along with a price tag that will be about a hundred times the cost of making it from scratch.

1 clove garlic, minced

¼ tsp salt, plus more as needed

3 grinds of fresh black pepper, plus more as needed

3 Tbsp apple cider vinegar

3 tsp honey

½ cup canola oil

To a small jar, add the garlic, salt, pepper, vinegar, honey, and oil and shake until emulsified. Taste and add more salt and pepper if needed. Store the vinaigrette in a lidded container in the fridge and use within 1 week.

PRAIRIE GRID SPICE BLEND

MAKES 2 CUPS

DC: Every home cook needs a go-to spice blend. Heck, every chef does too, and Scott Redekopp impressed us all during the 2018 Prairie Grid Dinner Series with this dynamic dry spice mix. It's now a mainstay in my pantry, so let's add it to yours as well.

"Consider this my version of an everything bagel seasoning mix or an 'alternative' to Montreal steak spice. It packs a punch when you use it to season all types of protein, but a little sprinkle on top of a salad or grilled vegetables will go a long way too. Make a batch and play around with it in the kitchen. You won't be disappointed." —Scott Redekopp, executive sous chef at Hotel Arts

2 Tbsp dried rosehips (see note)

2 Tbsp fennel seed

2 Tbsp Sichuan peppercorns

2 Tbsp coriander seed

2 Tbsp cumin seed, toasted and ground

3 whole star anise

7 Tbsp granulated sugar

7 Tbsp smoked salt

2 Tbsp dried minced garlic

2 Tbsp onion powder

2 Tbsp ground ginger

1 Tbsp ground cloves

Toast the rosehips, fennel seed, Sichuan peppercorns, coriander seed, cumin seed, and star anise in a small pan over medium-high heat for 2–3 minutes, shaking the pan periodically to help the spices toast evenly. Transfer to a food processor and grind until you have a fine, sand-like texture.

Combine the toasted ingredients with the sugar, salt, garlic, onion powder, ginger, and cloves in a medium bowl. Portion out into airtight containers and store in a cool, dry place for up to 6 months.

NOTE: *Rosehips aren't exclusive to the Prairies, but they are a favourite of many a chef who enjoys foraging. While chefs preserve rosehips in a multitude of ways, they are most accessible to home cooks in a dried format via speciality or online shops.*

COWBOY COUNTRY SPICE RUB

MAKES ½ CUP

TC: Ras el hanout is a spice mix found in North African recipes. The name is Arabic and translates to "head of the shop," referring to the top-shelf spices used to make the mixture. I'm partial to the President's Choice brand of ras el hanout because along with my three favourite spices (cardamom, star anise, and white pepper), the mix contains rose petal, which is fitting as that's our provincial flower in Alberta.

Combining ras el hanout with espresso and brown sugar adds both elegance and complexity to this rub, which works beautifully with red meats like beef and lamb. We're using coffee beans from a local roaster (always) to cozy up next to ras el hanout in this down-home, yet globally inspired, spice rub.

2 Tbsp ground espresso beans

2 Tbsp ras el hanout

2 Tbsp brown sugar

4 tsp kosher salt

Add all the ingredients to a bowl and whisk to combine. Transfer to a sealable container and keep in the cupboard for up to 3 months.

SIMPLE SYRUPS

A simple syrup is, simply, sugar and water, and it is used to add a sweet component that blends more easily into drinks than granulated sugar. Infusing a simple syrup with other ingredients like fruit, or even herbs or spices, adds flavour and thereby more dimension to the end product. Sometimes you make a more complex syrup without even knowing it; the liquid left over from the Spiced Cranberry Sauce (page 275) or the elixir from the Spiced Strawberries (page 61) is fantastic when used in cocktails, and the best part is, you're using something that might otherwise be discarded.

The measurements remain constant: 2 cups of fruit are added to 1 cup of sugar in 1 cup of water. The only difference is that when fruit is incorporated, we let it simmer a bit longer for flavour extraction.

BASIC SIMPLE SYRUP
MAKES 1⅓ CUPS

TC: Sometimes you need a syrup with no specific flavourings. The most basic of all requires two ingredients. It doesn't get much simpler than that.

1 cup granulated sugar
1 cup water

Combine the sugar and water in a small pot over medium heat and bring to a simmer. Reduce the heat to low and occasionally stir until the sweetener has completely dissolved, about 5 minutes. Transfer to a glass jar or bottle and store in the fridge for up to 1 month.

HASKAP SIMPLE SYRUP
MAKES 1½ CUPS

TC: While haskaps are becoming plentiful throughout the Prairies, you can find more of them across other parts of the country, and in the frozen foods section of grocery stores. The berry's flavour is a mashup of raspberry, blueberry, and a bit of concord grape and black currant. This recipe makes a gorgeous tangy dark-purple syrup that works well with clear spirits like gin, vodka, and tequila. We use it in our Haskap Smash (page 65).

2 cups fresh or frozen haskap berries

1 cup granulated sugar

1 cup water

Add the ingredients to a medium saucepan and bring to a boil. Turn the heat to low and simmer for 5 minutes. Take off the element and let cool. Strain the contents through a fine-mesh sieve into a glass jar and store in the fridge for up to 1 month.

RHUBARB SIMPLE SYRUP
MAKES 1½ CUPS

TC: While the colours of rhubarb can run the gamut from light green to dark red, choose the stalks that are rosy red to make this pretty-in-pink simple syrup. Rhubarb is all about the tang, with citrusy yet herbaceous flavour—there's nothing quite like it. We use this simple syrup in our Rosy Clover (page 66).

2 cups chopped rhubarb

1 cup granulated sugar

1 cup water

Add the ingredients to a medium saucepan and bring to a boil. Turn the heat to low and simmer for 5 minutes or until the sugar is dissolved and the rhubarb has broken down into a thick stew. Take off the element and let cool. Strain the contents through a fine-mesh sieve into a glass jar and store in the fridge for up to 1 month.

SPICED CRANBERRY SAUCE

MAKES 4 CUPS

TC: Are you really still using jellied cranberry sauce from a can? You won't be, after you try this recipe. The bonus is that you also get a couple of cups of cranberry simple syrup to use in cocktails. It plays particularly well with vodka or mulled wine.

4 cups fresh or frozen cranberries

2 cups granulated sugar

2 cups water

2 cinnamon sticks

1 or 2 star anise pods

3 strips orange peel

Juice of 1 orange

Add all of the ingredients to a medium saucepan and bring to a boil. Turn the heat down to medium-low and simmer for 15 minutes.

Pour the contents through a sieve with a bowl placed underneath to collect the liquid. The holes in the sieve should be of medium size to allow the cranberry seeds to pass through. Discard the cinnamon sticks, anise pods, and orange peel.

Rinse out the saucepan, then put the strained cranberries back in the pan and mash with a potato masher until the berries resemble a thick, chunky sauce. Store in a sealed container in the fridge for up to 1 month.

NOTE: *If using the syrup for drinks, pour the liquid through a fine-mesh sieve set over a bowl to remove any remaining seeds. Like the sauce, the syrup can be stored in the fridge in a sealed container for up to 1 month. Add the syrup to Prosecco or bourbon, and to Aperol for a negroni-esque cocktail sure to wow your guests during the holidays.*

PRAIRIE PRODUCERS AND SUPPLIERS: A BLACK BOOK

ALBERTA

Alchemist Vinegar

Anohka Distillery

Brant Lake Wagyu

The Butchery by Rge Rd

Chatsworth Farm

Empire Provisions

Field Notes Herbaceous
    Libations

Fifth Gen Gardens

Innisfail Growers

Knockout Heat Co.

Lakeside Farmstead

Meuwly's Artisan Food Market

Noble Premium Bison

Preserved

Reclaim Urban Farm

Saltcraft Meat Co.

Spragg's Meat Shop

Winter's Turkeys

Worthy Jams

MANITOBA

Chaeban Artisan Cheese

Flora & Farmer

Jardins St-Léon Gardens

Manitoba Harvest

New Iceland Fisheries

Oak Knoll Farm

Smak Dab Canadian Maple
    Mustard

Welchinski's Meats

Wild Man Ricing

SASKATCHEWAN

Be Magic

Black Fox Farm and Distillery

The Cure

Drake Meats

Living Sky Winery

Lucky Bastard Distillers

Meat Chops Snacks
    Canada Inc.

Northern Lights Foods

Nvigorate

Pine View Farms

River Stone

SaskMade Marketplace

Smokehaus Meats & Deli

Stumbletown Distilling

Three Farmers

THANK-YOUS

YOU CAN REALLY SPIN OUT on a regular basis when you're writing a cookbook—or any type of book, I'm sure. You're always wondering if you're forgetting one thing or if you've got too much of another. I *will* lose sleep at night wondering if I've forgotten a "thank-you" or two.

I first started food writing by way of Food Network Canada online in spring 2010. Catherine Jheon, the website's editor at the time, saw something special in me and by giving me a chance, got me started down a path of food, drink, and travel that led me to this book.

During this time, I was managing the long-standing Calgary coffeehouse Higher Ground. (Then) co-owners, Dave and Liane Hockey, were always encouraging my creativity and celebrating my successes. Years later, they continue to be supportive of the career that I've built. All the love and appreciation to you both.

I met Hanna Kassa in 2011 while on the programming board for a queer film festival in Calgary. We hit it off instantly and have remained pals ever since. Hanna helped me launch a non-profit cooking program for university students that would become somewhat of a catapult for my full-time food media career. Thank you, Hanna.

Twyla Campbell, *of course!* We've done so much together and share a love of the Prairies that few others do. Thanks for joining me for this project and the Prairie Grid Dinner Series.

Mairlyn Smith, you have never wavered in your support of my (occasionally quirky) projects and me over the years. Mentor, friend, fancy gala dinner date . . . whatever role I look to you for, you fill it seamlessly. You mean the world to me, and this book would not have come to life without your support.

Carmen Cheng, while we have had plenty of fun times together, what I value most about you is your kindness to everyone and your thoughtful perspectives. I approach the way I cook, dine, and write differently because of you . . . and it's all for the better.

To all of the Prairie Grid Dinner Series alumni from 2017 to today, while not all of you have recipes in this book, you all inspire me. There are so many reasons why I love the Prairies, and seeing passionate chefs and restaurateurs like you create and innovate is a huge component of that love.

Dong Kim, thanks for always having a great eye and attention to detail, especially when I was feeling burnt out, frustrated, or defeated . . . or all three. Also, thanks to Ken Hughes for providing us with some Prairie landscape shots for this book.

As well, a thank-you to the multi-talented Alex Hughes for always being up for cooking a recipe from this book. I appreciate you!

Jenn McCurry at Pepo Ceramics for all of the stunning plateware that appears in many photos in this cookbook. I couldn't imagine my plateware collection looking any other way than how it does with your beautiful creations tucked into my kitchen cupboards.

Sending out love to my friends who often have to remind me that life isn't solely about cooking "gourmand" at home or dining out at "cool" restaurants. To my partner Jace Racette, Desiree Schultz, Adria Britton, Annie Hanson, Matt Bangsund, Jenn Kwan, Kenny Kwan, Kerry Bennett, Ryan Massel, Rob Gairns, Jamie Penno, and others: I love you all.

To Robert McCullough at Appetite by Random House, thank you for believing in this idea and letting Twyla and me bring it to fruition. There is so much to share when it comes to the Prairies food and drink scene, so we appreciate being the tip of the iceberg with this book. To our book editor Rachel Brown and the rest of the team at Appetite, I can only imagine that it isn't easy to work with one author on editing a huge manuscript, let alone two on the same book with different stylistic approaches. Thank you for merging Twyla's words and culinary creations with mine and helping create a cohesive celebration of Prairie cooking.

It goes without saying that there are so many producers and agricultural boards that helped support our recipe development process and travels to make this book possible. In particular, thank you to Canada Beef, Alberta Pulse, and Canadian Hemp Trade Alliance.

Last, but not least, thanks to all of the readers who have made it all the way to the end of our book to read the "thank-yous" section. I appreciate you too!

—Dan

PRAIRIE TOOK A WAGONLOAD OF people to shift it from an ambitious idea to this tangible thing you now hold in your hands. I say "ambitious" because that is Dan Clapson's resting state. Dan doesn't do easy or slow or small (or one thing at a time) . . . and that's okay.

So, my first words of gratitude are for my fellow food-writing friend: thank you, Dan, for asking me to partner with you on this beautiful book. Keep throwing those ideas against the wall, no matter how ambitious (read: wild, hairbrained, or monumental) they may sound. Somehow, they always work out.

To the Appetite Random House team and Rachel Brown, our editor, thank you for keeping us on task while guiding us through this project. Thanks for believing in what we've known for years—that what we have here on the Prairies is very special. I'm so proud to show off this body of work under the Penguin Random House name.

Dong Kim, your photography skill and patience saved us so many times, I've lost count. I have immense gratitude to the dedication you showed towards this project. A million heart-felt thank-yous for going the extra mile(s) time and time again.

I couldn't even begin to express my thanks to the hard-working producers we have on the Prairies, many of whom have become my friends. Your generosity with product helped us immensely and I'm so proud to have a hand in showcasing what you make and grow to the rest of Canada.

To the friends I leaned on for encouragement throughout this process, you have my love and appreciation. I have an extraordinary council—you know who you are. Thanks for your encouragement and for listening and not falling asleep while I rambled on about everything, even the non-food-related stuff.

And, to my family—my siblings for making me laugh and sharing memories of the food we grew up eating and what an extraordinary cook our mom was, and to my daughters, Erin and Paige, for cheering me on and inspiring me, again—you have all of my heart, and more.

—Twyla

INDEX